What to SEE in Palm Springs

What
to
SEE
in
Palm
Springs

LOCAL TOUR GUIDE TELLS ALL
Sights, History & Stories

John Stark

ISBN: 979-8-86705235-5

Published by: John Stark

Printed in the United States of America

First Edition

Materials used in 'What to See in Palm Springs' include photos or other images provided under license by the Palm Springs Historical Society. The Society is not responsible for uses made by any licensee of such Images, and a licensee's publication or other use of these images should not be construed as the Society's endorsement of any work in which they appear, including 'What to See in Palm Springs'

Photos by John Stark. Additional photos by Chris Cole and Henry Lehn. Front and back cover photos by Henry Lehn

Book and jacket design by Daniel Baum / b2creative.us
Typography by Daniel Baum

whattoseeinps@gmail.com

To Zaddie Bunker, who taught me you don't need an airplane to fly

-John Stark

Contents

Introduction

To see — to really see — Palm Springs, you can be your own guide. In your own car. You can be informed and knowledgeable. Through this book, I will escort you all over this famous resort town. You will not just be going sightseeing; you will learn about the history and importance of the sites you are seeing.

I am a tour guide who lives full-time in Palm Springs. I have been giving tours since residing here in 2018 and even owned my own tour company. I'm also a lifelong newspaper and magazine journalist. As a veteran journalist, I believe in truth, accuracy and research. For every site, I will tell you its location, history and importance. Some descriptions are short; others are essays. Many are sites that only locals know about. Each is accompanied by images.

This book is not about trendy places to eat, drink or party. It goes right to the heart of Palm Springs. With a few exceptions, all the sites in this book are free to visit and to look at. You can easily see them from your car window and, in most cases, you can get out of your car for a closer look. I've confined most every site to Palm Springs city limits.

Fewer and fewer tourists today know of any of the great stars who once lived here. Even though Palm Springs is not the celebrity playground it once was, it is home to their ever-present spirits. Many of our streets and highways are named after those glamorous stars. Once when I asked for directions, I was told, "Take Bob Hope to Frank Sinatra, cross Gerald Ford and Ginger Rogers, but if you hit Dinah Shore, you've gone too far."

The most noted stars of Palm Springs today are our architects, both living and deceased. Since the early years of the 20th century architects, designers and builders, have been drawn to Palm Springs to set their imaginations free on this sandy canvas. I was privileged to interview several for this book. We are, after all, the modernism capital of the world.

When I give tours by van, bus or foot, I've limited time to talk about our visionary pioneers, especially the strong women, feminists before their time. Women who found their way here could shape their own destinies, dream big, fly airplanes, ride with the Indians. In the 1950s, the Agua Caliente Band of the Cahuilla Indians had a five-member, all-woman tribal council, a first in America. Most tourists are surprised to learn that half of our 94.68 square miles is tribal land. The Agua Caliente have called Palm Springs home for thousands of years. Our canyons and mountains are sacred ground.

I've included personal observations about the sites and people who live here. First off, those who stay through the summer are called "desert rats." I am in that exclusive company. I tell a few show-biz stories, too. Indulge me.

Just know that when you take this book in your car, you are taking me along, too.

About Me

I am a native Californian, born in Los Angeles. Growing up, my father would take our family on outings to the Salton Sea in our Ford Woody. In those days, you could play on its beaches and swim in its waters. You could roll down the shifting sand dunes that once lined Highway 111, a giddy experience I've never forgotten. Palm Springs today is not so different from the Palm Springs I knew then. The modernist houses have been restored, looking as if they'd just been built. Vintage cars with shiny chrome fenders are on the road again. A popular radio station, 107.3 Mod FM, plays the hits of the 50s and 60s all day long. Many of my generation have come to Palm Springs to redefine themselves as cooler versions of their parents. Like most people here, I also came for the weather. As Bob Dylan said, "You don't have to shovel sunshine."

How to Use This Book

I have put all of the sites in alphabetical order, starting with their first names, from Abraham Lincoln to Zaddie Bunker. At the back of the book is a map of Palm Springs. I've included Fun Facts, Un-Fun Facts, Fact Checking, Personal Notes and Detours, the later taking you to related sites reachable by car. I've denoted sidebars by colorful asterisks, like this: ✳

Acknowledgements

Thank you to Renee Brown, director of education and associate creator at the Palm Springs Historical Society, for answering my many questions and helping with photo selections. Thank you to PSHS President Tracy Conrad for her informative stories in the Desert Sun newspaper. Thank you to Kate Anderson, publicity director of the Agua Caliente Band of Cahuilla Indians, for also answering my questions and taking my book to the Tribal Council to vet for facts.

A huge thank you to artist-photographer Henry Lehn and Patti Patton-Lehn. From color corrections to maps to front and back covers, I could not have finished this book without the two of you. Thank you to proofreader Lee Barnathan for his eagle eye, and to book designer Dan Baum, whose creativity (and patience) skillfully put all the moving parts together. Thank you to Jennifer Lee Pryor for her generosity and encouragement and for bringing me Joey, my rescued senior shepherd. To longtime friend Kathy Mandry for her editorial guidance. To Barbara Bordnick for her photographic advice. To artists Raj Bharadia and Patrick Kelly for their sketches and friendship and to longtime friends Will Hopkins and Mary K Baumann for their involvement.

Thank you to expert bus driver Gary Ramey, who got me started as a tour guide. Thank you to Celebrity Tours' Tim and Celia Bannister for entrusting me with their vans. I'm very grateful to Jay Dougherty for his time and legal advice. Grateful as well to Mickey and Suzanne Lang, lifelong Palm Springs residents who shared with me their stories and boxes of memorabilia. And thank you to Bill Swindle, for just being Bill Swindle.

A special bow to Grammy Award-winning radio announcer Don Wardell at 107.3 Mod FM. Thank you for letting me come on your radio show every Monday afternoon at the Agua Caliente Casino's Cascade Lounge to share my stories. A collective thank you to the wonderful friends I've met there.

Thank you to Palm Springs architects James Cioffi, Chris Mills and Hugh Kaptur for sharing their visions with me. You have enriched this book.

Thank you to Palm Springs.

Chris Cole

Chris Cole, my neighbor's tech-savvy grandson, has been a part of this book since its conception. He has experience in cinematography, photography, website design and social media marketing. He and his father, Chris Sr., are political consultants for local- and state-elected offices across California. Born and reared in Palm Springs, Chris helped me with the book's photography and electronic files, and without him there would be no book. Chris is currently studying marketing at the University of Nevada, Reno.

Brief History

Before checking out Palm Springs, you might want to read about how our city came about. When I give tours, I always start with this information.

Palm Springs is unlike almost any other city in that it's a checkerboard of tribal and private lands; each parcel is one square mile. This checkerboard was laid out in the 1860s by the federal government to encourage Southern Pacific Railroad to build a route through the Coachella Valley as part of a transcontinental line. The federal government, as a financial incentive, granted the railroad 10 miles of odd-numbered sections of land on each side of the railroad right of way, which today parallels Interstate 10. The even sections were given in trust to the Agua Caliente Indians. Agua Caliente means "hot water" in Spanish.

President Ulysses S. Grant established the present Agua Caliente Band of Cahuilla Indians' reservation in 1876. and expanded it in 1877. It was at this time that this tribe was separated from the other eight Cahuilla tribes in Southern California. Since the land was given to the Agua Caliente in trust, they couldn't own or develop it. The reservation land remained in trust until 1949, following decades of legal challenges from the Agua Caliente. President Dwight Eisenhower signed the Equalization Law in 1959, which allowed U.S. tribes to profit from their properties. The Agua Caliente were then able to secure 99-year leases on their land, lifting them out of poverty.

Today, the Agua Caliente Reservation consists of 31,680 acres that span across the desert in a checkerboard pattern within three cities (Palm Springs, Cathedral City and Rancho Mirage) and into the Santa Rosa and San Jacinto mountains. Sixty-seven hundred of these acres are in Palm Springs, making this tribe the single largest landowner in Palm Springs. As a sovereign nation, the 400-or-so-member tribe is exempt from city, state and federal taxes. The U.S. Supreme Court in 1987 granted American Indians sovereignty over their lands, meaning they could do what they want with them. This led to the Indian Gaming Regulatory Act and the building of casinos. The Agua Caliente Tribe has three casinos — one each in Palm Springs, Rancho Mirage and Cathedral City.

Generally, anyone can own a home or building on the reservation, just not hold title to the land itself — instead, one pays rent to an Agua Caliente land-owner for use of the land. Rents can be raised or lowered by the tribe when they are renewed. The length of a lease doesn't matter if you're paying cash, though the resale buyer pool can be limited. To obtain a 30-year home loan, there needs to be 35 years left on the lease.

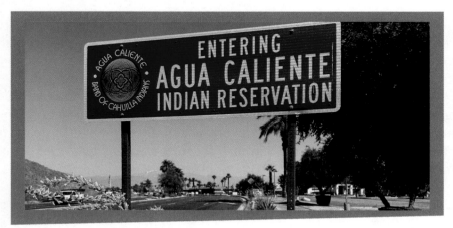

When you're visiting Palm Springs, you are also visiting the Agua Caliente reservation and are constantly traveling from U.S. to tribal land.

Palm Springs is located in California's Sonoran Desert, in Riverside County. We are the northernmost city in the Coachella Valley. The other cities are Desert Hot Springs, Thousand Palms, Cathedral City, Rancho Mirage, Palm Desert, Indian Wells, La Quinta, Indio and Coachella. The name Coachella comes from a misspelling of the valley's old name, Conchilla, from a Spanish word meaning "little shell" that referenced the fossil shells found in the area. The first "a" in Coachella isn't pronounced.

Palm Springs has a total area of 95 square-miles and is sheltered by the San Bernardino Mountains to the north, the Santa Rosa Mountains to the south, by the San Jacinto Mountains to the west and by the Little San Bernardino Mountains to the east. Our elevation is 480 feet above sea level. Being a re-sort city, our population varies from 45,000 to double that in the fall, winter and spring months. On average, we get about 5 1/2 inches of rain a year. Daytime temperatures are warm-to-hot most of the year, though nights can be chilly. Our coldest month is December, with an average high of 69 degrees Fahrenheit. Summer's can be brutal with daytime temps in the triple digits.

Chronology

* 1850: California becomes a state.
* 1876: President Grant establishes Indian reservations across the Coachella Valley.
* 1884: John Guthrie McCallum, his wife and four children become the first permanent, non-Indian family in Palm Springs.
* 1876: First railroad line through the Coachella Valley completed.
* 1886: Dr. Welwood Murray opens the Palm Springs Hotel, the first inn and health resort.
* 1893-94: A 21 -day record rainfall is followed by an 11-year drought, wiping out crops and irrigation ditches and driving homesteaders away.
* 1909: Nellie Coffman opens the Desert Inn.
* 1916: First paved highway opens in Palm Springs, which connects the village with Banning, 22.5 miles to the west.
* 1919: First Anglo child, Ted McKinney, is born in Palm Springs.
* 1927: Tom O'Donnell builds the first golf course in the Coachella Valley.
* 1938: The City of Palm Springs is incorporated. Phillip L. Boyd becomes the first mayor.
* 1938: Palm Springs Fire Department is formed.
* 1939: Public library and high school open.
* 1939: The U.S. Army purchases the El Mirador Hotel and turns it into a 1,600-bed general hospital to treat troops returning from overseas.
* 1944: U.S. Supreme Court allows Indians to own their land.
* 1954: President and First Lady Mamie Eisenhower make their first trip to the Coachella Valley, spending several days at Smoke Tree Ranch.
* 1956: New City Hall, designed by Alfred Frey, opens.
* 1958: City purchases land from Agua Caliente Indians for present-day airport.
* 1959: The Indian Long-Term Leasing Act is signed by President Eisenhower, which permits the Agua Caliente to lease their lands for up to 99 years.
* 1960: Bob Hope Classic founded. First winner is Arnold Palmer.
* 1962: President John F. Kennedy visits Palm Springs.
* 1963: Palm Springs Aerial Tramway opens.
* 1987: Indians allowed casinos in California.
* 1988: Sony Bono elected mayor.
* 1990: Palm Springs International Film Festival debuts.
* 1991: Thursday night VillageFest Street Fair begins.
* 1992: Downtown Walk of Stars is created.
* 1992: First Pride parade.
* 1994: First Festival of Lights Parade.
* 1996: Palm Springs Air Museum opens on Nov. 11, Veterans Day.
* 1998: U.S. Congressman Sony Bono killed in skiing accident.
* 2006: First annual Veterans Day Parade.
* 2021: "Forever Marilyn" statue returns to Palm Springs.

What to SEE in Palm Springs

Abraham Lincoln's Reclining Profile

266-278 North Palm Canyon Drive, Downtown

Abraham Lincoln in Palm Springs? Laying back and getting some rays? Many visitors and residents walk right by Henry Frank Arcade on North Palm Canyon Drive, across from the Hyatt Hotel, not knowing about the boutique shops that are housed therein. Check out what's at the end of the courtyard: An antique pipe telescope that's aimed directly at the San Jacinto Mountains. Look through it — go on, it's free — and you'll see a reclined, naturally occurring profile of our 16th president. You can best see Abe at sundown. The telescope was commissioned in the 1920s by the Hotel La Palma, which was at this site. It was hoped Lincoln would attract customers.

> **SIGHTSEEING TIP:** The best spot to see Lincoln is, however, at the intersection of Belardo and Andreas roads, across from Downtown Park, at sundown or shortly before. At this location, you won't need a telescope or binoculars.

✳ CHECK OUT

...what's at the end of the Henry Frank Arcade courtyard: An antique pipe telescope that's aimed directly at the San Jacinto Mountains.

- Abraham Lincoln's Reclining Profile -

Agua Caliente Tribal Administration
5401 Dinah Shore Drive, East Palm Springs

The brawny building sporting the floor-to-ceiling windows on Dinah Shore Drive, just past Gene Autry Trail heading east, is the Agua Caliente Band of Cahuilla Indians Tribal Administration Plaza. This is where the Tribal Council's governing body makes laws and implements the directions voted up by tribal membership. Its nation's flag, flying between the United States and California flags, depicts a woven basket. The Agua Caliente's name for their reservation is Sec-he, which means "boiling water." The Spanish translated Sec-he to Agua Caliente. Since the late 1900s, the Agua Caliente have been an independent band of the Desert Cahuilla Tribe, which has inhabited the Coachella Valley for more than 3,000 years.

- Agua Caliente Tribal Administration -

Agua Caliente Casino Palm Springs
401 East Amado Road, Midtown

The Agua Caliente Casino Palm Springs opened in 1995 and since then has doubled down, adding two more casinos, one in Rancho Mirage and another in Cathedral City. All have Class Three status, meaning that besides card games, Bingo, slot machine and Lotto, they can offer Nevada-style games, too, such as Blackjack and Baccarat. This casino is more than 45,000 square feet and is open 24 hours. Gambling became legal on tribal lands shortly after Congress passed the Indian Gaming Regulatory Act in 1987. The Act has served as a means of generating revenue for tribes across the country. Before 1987, many members of the Agua Caliente Tribe were living in harsh conditions. Today, not so. Some 400 tribal members share the profits of the casinos, making this one of the nation's wealthiest tribes. Tribal members living on reservations are not subject to federal, state and city income tax, and tribal casinos do not pay corporate income tax. Smoking is allowed in the casino.

It was under the three-decade leadership of the late Tribal Chairman Richard Milanovich that living conditions for the tribe changed drastically. Milanovich helped usher in the casinos, which brought the tribe wealth and political clout. Yet according to his 2012 obituary in the Los Angeles Times, Milanovich never saw casino profits as a panacea. He advocated tribal members to look beyond comfortable lifestyles. "They will still have to become viable, working members of society," he told the Times in a 1990 interview. The Agua Caliente gives generously to dozens of local non-profits, including Desert AIDS Project, the Mizel Center, the Barbara Sinatra Children's Center and to fire departments in Palm Springs and Cathedral City.

- Agua Caliente Casino -

Agua Caliente Cultural Plaza
100 North Indian Canyon Drive, Midtown

The Agua Caliente Cultural Plaza is a newer addition to Palm Springs, opening in early 2023. It features a museum that celebrates the tribe's history and culture, nature walks and a spa with a natural hot spring. This site was a nine-acre, washingtonia filifera palm tree oasis where the Agua Caliente lived for thousands of years, except in the summer months when they relocated to higher elevations and cooler canyons. The ancestors of the Agua Caliente Tribe relied on the Agua Caliente hot mineral springs for fresh water for bathing, ritual and community. In the late 1800, visitors, mostly white, began making treks to the spring for its healing and restorative powers. Call it the first tourist attraction in Palm Springs. Over time, bath houses opened on the site. The new Spa at Séc-he (which means "boiling water" in the Cahuilla language) is the site's fifth bathhouse. The actual spring of 26 gallons a minute and at about 105 degrees bubbles up from a cavern a mile and a half below with steadfast regularity. It is preserved and contained in a new collection tank with a pumping system to the new spa, which is open to the public.

The Museum and Cultural Plaza's main entrance resembles a woven basket as the Agua Caliente women are heralded for their basket weaving skills and pottery. The tribe's flag also depicts a basket. The Cultural Museum was previously located at the Village Green on South Palm Canyon Drive. The new museum puts an even brighter light on the Agua Caliente Indians's history, culture, traditions, modern-day life and contributions.

> PERSONAL NOTE: In 2014, the Spa Hotel was razed to make way for the Cultural Plaza. Preservationists were not happy about that, as the mid-century structure was designed by noted modernists William F. Cody and Donald Wexler. Palm Springs preservation laws do not apply to tribal lands. I do think, however, the Cultural Plaza is a beautiful and important addition to our downtown.

- Agua Caliente Cultural Plaza -

Alan Ladd Hardware Store
500 South Palm Canyon Drive, Financial District

The big bear of a building with the soaring windows at the corner of Ramon Road and South Palm Canyon Drive was founded by movie star **Alan Ladd,** best remembered for playing the gunslinger Shane in the 1953 western. Ladd was frustrated by the nearby Builders Supply hardware store at 490 East Sunny Dunes Road because it wouldn't deliver merchandise he had purchased for his modernist house in Las Palmas. So, just like Shane, Ladd took matters into his own hands. In 1955, he commissioned his own hardware store and named it after himself. He even showed up every day to help the crew build it. The Alan Ladd Hardware Store was in business for 47 years, long after the actor's death in 1964. It was a hardware store in tune with its well-to-do clientele, selling Baccarat crystal and sequined screwdrivers. The three-tiered building was designed by mid-century architects Donald Wexler and Richard Harrison. It's now the 500, an office complex.

PERSONAL NOTE: When passing by this building on a tour, I ask people if they know who Alan Ladd was. Most say yes, that he was married to Betty White. Wrong answer. That was "Password" game-show host Allen Ludden. I often get asked if Alan Ladd was married to Cheryl Ladd of "Charlie's Angels" fame. That was Alan Ladd Jr., son of Alan Ladd.

- Alan Ladd Hardware Store -

❊ SHOWDOWN AT BUILDERS SUPPLY

Alan Ladd in a scene from 'Shane.'

FUN FACT

At 5 feet, 6 inches, Alan Ladd was one of Hollywood's shortest leading men. To make him appear taller on screen, doorknobs were placed lower on doors.

❊ ALAN LADD ESTATE
323 Camino Norte West, Las Palmas

It was in this five-bed, five-bath Donald Wexler-designed house that actor Alan Ladd died in 1964 at the of 50. He overdosed on a mixture of pills and alcohol. Accidental death or suicide? Two years earlier, he shot himself in the chest with a revolver. At age 12, his mother died in front of him after swallowing rat poison.

- Alan Ladd Hardware Store -

Aluminaire House
Palm Springs Art Museum, 101 North Museum Dr., Historic Tennis District

Rendering by Raj Bharadia

The three-story steel structure that's next to the Palm Springs Art Museum is the legendary Aluminaire House, the first house made entirely of metal. It was designed in 1931 for a Manhattan architectural exhibition by the visionary architects, Swiss-born Alfred Frey, the father of Palm Springs desert modernism, and A. Lawrence Kocher. The original price tag was $1,000, a steal. Constructed mostly of aluminum and glass components, the five-room, 1200-square-foot house was intended to be mass-produced and affordable to the average worker — assembly time just three days, faster than putting together an IKEA bookcase. Over the decades, the Aluminaire House had been disassembled and reassembled on various owners' properties. Years of fundraising and planning eventually got the house to our art museum for permanent display (see: Wexler Steel Houses).

- Aluminaire House -

Amtrak Station
North Indian Canyon Drive & Palm Springs Station Road

The Palm Springs train depot is located seven miles north of downtown. There is no scheduled bus or taxi service to and from it. The station has no waiting room, is unmanned and has no wheelchairs if you need one. Amtrak's Sunset Limited and Texas Eagle offer thrice-weekly passenger service in both directions, arriving in the middle of the night. Should you choose to walk to your hotel upon arrival here, you'll have to brave the strong winds that howl through the San Gorgonio Pass and that power the windmills. North Indian Canyon Drive, the main road to and from town, is often closed due to blinding sandstorms. The sign at the train depot says, "Welcome to Palm Springs" when it should read, "Good Luck."

SITESEEKING TIP:
The Amtrak Station is the best place to see the windmills from inside or outside of your car.

The former depot, built in 1934, was demolished in 1970, thus ending the theatrics of arrival. The current, no-frills station opened in 1997 and was designed to blend into the desert landscape.

- Amtrak Station -

Andreas, Murray & Palm Canyons
Indian Canyons

When giving a tour, I often ask if anyone has heard of these adjoining canyons, which are bold, beautiful and full of surprises, the way nature likes it. I'm always surprised at how many tourists are unaware of their existence. Located at the southern end of the Indian Canyons neighborhood, they are three of Palm Springs's five sacred canyons (Chino and Tahquitz Canyons are the other two). To get there, take South Palm Canyon Drive all the way to the end, driving (or biking) past ranch lands and stables. Shortly after crossing Murray Canyon Drive, you'll come to a gated kiosk, which is the entrance. There is a fee per visitor. Once inside, parking is free. Pets, no. Horses, yes.

This is tribal land that's owned and operated by the Agua Caliente Band of Cahuilla Indians. Ancestors of the Agua Caliente have lived in these canyons for thousands of years, where food, water and shelter were plentiful. In the 1800s, Europeans trickled into the area, foreshadowing a struggle for control of this natural wonder by such forces as the U.S. government, Southern Pacific Railroad, hotel developers, hunters, basket collectors and tourists. Juan Andreas (1874-1959) dedicated his life to his tribe's right to hold onto these canyons.

- Andreas, Murray & Palm Canyons -

Andreas Canyon

Once past the entrance booth, follow the signs to Andreas Canyon trailhead, which is a mile down the road. Approaching it, you'll see an oasis of skirted washingtonia filifera palm trees, also known as California fan palms and desert fan palms, that are dramatically imposed on the desert landscape. They look surreal, as oases do. Of Andreas, Murray and Palm Canyons, Andreas is the only one with a running stream. Park in the parking lot and check things out. There are benches and picnic tables shaded by the indigenous palms. Dip your toes in the cold stream water, which comes from the snowmelt flowing down the San Jacinto Mountains. Through lab tests, the Agua Caliente monitor this water resource to safeguard it. Just off the parking lot is Pride Rock, an impressive, natural sculpture. Here, you can see bedrock mortars and stone metates used centuries ago by Indian women for grinding plants.

- Andreas, Murray & Palm Canyons -

If you feel inclined, you can hike the Andreas trail, which is mostly flat and only a mile round trip. As you look skyward, try not to think of earthquakes as you gaze at the gigantic boulders balancing precariously atop steep cliffs formed by seismic action. Halfway through the looping trail, you will find a fence that

- Andreas, Murray & Palm Canyons -

has signs saying, "Andreas Canyon Club" and "No Trespassing." Looking through the fence, you get a view of Palm Springs's most mystifying, secretive complex: 22 rock houses that blend so perfectly with the steep canyon walls that they almost disappear. This is not part of the tribal lands. The primitive structures were designed by architect Lee Miller, who also built the Araby Cove rock houses (see: Rock Houses). The Andreas Canyon Club was formed in 1921 by conservation-minded Los Angeles businessmen. Walt Disney wanted to be a member but was turned down because of the attention he would bring.

There's no vehicle access to Murray Canyon, which was named for Palm Springs pioneer Dr. Welwood Murray. From the Andreas Canyon picnic area, you can access hiking trails to the canyon. From Murray Canyon, a four-mile round-trip hike leads to the Seven Sisters, a collection of waterfalls.

- Andreas, Murray & Palm Canyons -

Next stop: Palm Canyon

Driving east out of Andreas Canyon, turn right when you hit the access road. This will take you south to Palm Canyon, three miles away. On the journey, you'll pass the remains of a gas station before driving through Split Rock. Buses and oversized vehicles cannot squeeze through these imposing boulders, so you have to park and walk the short distance to Palm Canyon. Driving up a hill, you'll come to a parking area where there's a souvenir shop. From here, you get a sweeping view of the lower part of the Palm Canyon Oasis, which extends for 15 miles. Containing thousands of washingtonia fillifera, it's the world's largest oases of this variety of palm tree. You can hike down to it.

- Andreas, Murray & Palm Canyon -

detour

Another great place to experience an oasis with desert palm trees is the Coachella Valley Preserve in Thousand Palms, which is managed by the U.S. Fish and Wildlife Service. A mile-long round-trip walk takes you through several sheltered oases. To get there from Palm Springs, take Ramon Road going east and turn left at Varner Road. It's a 25-minute car trip; longer by camel or palanquin. It's free to visit but please leave a donation and no pets allowed. Endangered desert pupfish live in these ponds. Pupfish are three-inch fish whose lineage goes back to the Ice Age when the desert was under water. They have adapted to extreme weather conditions. Over the years, visitors to the preserve have been introducing non-native species to the ponds such as red crawfish, which eat the pupfish. In a government effort to save the pupfish, the preserve was closed for two years before reopening in the fall of 2022. The project was 100% successful in getting rid of non-indigenous water creatures. But then one night, a well-meaning do-gooder dumped buckets of pupfish into the ponds. Unfortunately, they weren't the same species of pupfish unique to these ponds. Researchers can't tell one species from the other.

SAN ANDREAS FAULT

Where can you go to see the San Andreas Fault line? The best place, and the closest, is the Coachella Valley Preserve. There is a sign pointing to a path that can get you up close and on top of it. The north branch of the San Andreas Fault runs through Desert Hot Springs, while the south branch cuts across North Palm Springs and the north side of Thousand Palms.

- Andreas, Murray & Palm Canyons -

(Photo by Barbara Bordnick)

SHAKEN NOT STIRRED: My friend, Jason, who's in his late 30s and was born and raised here, told me he'd never had a martini, Palm Springs' signature cocktail. "I don't get their appeal," he told me. Seeing as it was nearing 5 p.m., I fixed him one, which I served in a classic martini glass with two olives on a toothpick. Sitting on a barstool at my kitchen island, he took his first sip. As he did, we heard what sounded like a sonic boom. My kitchen lurched forward and back again, the result of a strong tremor. "Wow," Jason said, "now I get it!"

- Andreas, Murray & Palm Canyons -

Araby Cove/Palm Canyon Wash
East Palm Canyon Drive, South Palm Springs

The neighborhood you see looking west from the bridge over the Palm Canyon Wash on East Palm Canyon Drive is Araby Cove, an amalgamation of houses in every kind of style, era, color, and size, each a unique specimen, including what's left of three Rock Houses (see: Rock Houses). Because Araby Canyon borders a wildlife preserve residents have reported finding wild animals cooling off in their swimming pools. There are two entrances to Araby Cove as you're heading south on East Palm Canyon Drive: South Araby Drive and Rim

Road. South Araby Drive is on the north side of the bridge and Rim Road on the south side. The two roads eventually connect so you can travel one road in and another out. Teetering on the rocky ridge above Araby Canyon is the exclusive Southridge neighborhood where Bob Hope's monumental house is, and where such mid-century celebrities as William Holden and Steve McQueen once owned houses.

The Palm Canyon Wash cuts through Araby Canyon like an unpaved freeway, running east from the San Jacinto Mountains to its confluence with the Whitewater River. The wash can best be viewed and accessed from the end of Barona Road at the south end of the Smoke Tree Village Shopping

The opening to the Palm Canyon Wash levee (above). The levee is a great place to walk a dog. You'll find doggie bags at the gate. I bring my dog, Joey, there.

Center on East Palm Canyon Drive. (Barona Road is the southern extension of Farrell Drive.) Few tourists know about the mile-long Barona Road, which dead ends at the wash. You can park your car here and access the levee through an open gate. From atop the levee you'll have sweeping, photo-op views of Araby Cove, the Rock Houses and Southridge. Looking north, you'll have commanding views of central Palm Springs all the way to the windmills. Take a short stroll west on the levee and you'll get a voyeuristic look into the Smoke Tree Ranch colony. On the following page I've marked with arrows the Southridge houses where celebrities lived and that you can see from the levee.

UN-FUN FACT

The wash is a great area to walk, run and hike. Just know that if there's a downpour the dry riverbed can behave like a drunk college kid at spring break. Nearly four inches of rain fell in a two-hour span on Valentine's Day, 2019, flooding roads into and out of Araby Canyon, nearly washing away houses.

- Araby Cove/Palm Canyon Wash/South Palm Springs -

The house that's the farthest to the right belonged to the late Suzanne Somers, who died Oct. 15, 2023. The "Three's Company" star bought the four-bedroom, 4.5-bathroom house for $2.35 million in 2020. She and husband Alan Hammel wanted to downsize from their 70-acre, French-style villa, which is located on a steep and rocky mountainside in The Mesa neighborhood. You can't drive up to that estate. You need to either hike or take a funicular.

Looking left from Somers's abode, you'll come to a long, flat-roofed house. This was William Holden's second home in Palm Springs. Holden commissioned this house in 1977 from **architect Hugh Kaptur** and lived there with actress Stefanie Powers. To the right of the house is a platform that's perched over a cliff. It sported one of Holden's Asian sculptures. Kaptur didn't want to build the platform, fearing someone could fall off it. Ironically, an intoxicated

- Araby Cove/Palm Canyon Wash/South Palm Springs -

William Holden's house upon completion. (Photograph courtesy of the Palm Springs Historical Society - All Rights Reserved)

Holden died from a fall in 1981, in the bedroom of his Santa Monica residence. The 62-year-old star hit his head on a bedside table and bled to death. Alison Janey owned the house from 2006-2012.

"I originally wanted the house to have a pitched, sloping roof that would resemble a thatched roof," Kaptur told me. "Holden didn't want that. He was insistent on a flat roof so that when he drove up to the house he could get a sweeping, unobstructed view of the mountains."

The big house on the precipice to the left of Holden's belonged to the late John and Eunice Johnson, the founding publishers of Jet and Ebony magazines. In 1982, John Johnson became the first African American to be on the Forbes 400 list. President Clinton awarded him the Presidential Medal of Freedom. The house, built in 1974, boasts two swimming pools, one being an infinity pool at the far left corner of the cliff. The other pool is in an inner courtyard. In 2019, the Johnson Publishing Company filed for bankruptcy (blame it on the Internet). To raise money, the Johnsons' daughter, Linda Rice

- Araby Cove/Palm Canyon Wash/South Palm Springs -

Alfred Elrod's copper-roof domed house (left) and Steve McQueen's modern house (right) can be best viewed from the Palm Canyon Wash levee.

Johnson, sold the house. She also auctioned off the historic Ebony-Jet photo archives that chronicled black American life for 76 years. The photos sold for some $40 million to four public institutions, including the Ford Foundation and the Smithsonian.

Looking east, a little way down from the Johnson house, is a two-toned copper roof that resembles a circus tent. This house belonged to interior designer Alfred Elrod. The house was built by architect John Lautner and was the prototype for Bob Hope's bigger house up the street. It was used in the 1971 James Bond film, Diamonds are Forever. It's where the diamond-smuggling villain, William Whyte, lived. He was played by country-western singer turned sausage king, Jimmy Dean — not to be confused with James Dean.

To the right of Elrod's is a minimalist looking house that has large glass windows and a white side wall. Steve McQueen lived here in the 1970s with his second wife, Ali McGraw. They liked motorcycles and dune buggies, which they'd race up and down the hillsides, stirring up dust and neighbors' tempers. When Bob Hope's house caught fire just before completion, McQueen organized an unsuccessful bucket brigade.

- Araby Cove/Palm Canyon Wash/South Palm Springs -

Architecture and Design Center

300 South Palm Canyon Drive at Belardo Road, Downtown

At the Palm Springs Art Museum's Architecture and Design Center, you'll find the original blueprints to many of Palm Springs's modernist houses and businesses, period photographs, a bookstore celebrating the modernist era and special exhibitions. Originally the Santa Fe Savings and Loan, the center, completed in 1961, was designed by E. Stewart Williams. With its elevated base, thin support beams and glass windows, this building purposely appears to be hovering above the ground as if it were about to take off. But since it has Class 1 Historical Preservation status, it's staying.

Richard Neutra

✳ CHECK OUT

...the architects who have stars on the Walk of Fame out front include Albert Frey, Hugh Kaptur, Donald Wexler and Paul R. Williams.

- Architecture and Design Center -

Arenas District

East Arenas Road between Indian Canyon & Palm Canyon drives, Downtown

At barely a block long, Arenas Road is bulging with gay businesses, from a shop selling the latest in bear wear to Hunters, where guys sporting chiseled, Mount Jacinto-like torsos dance shirtless on Fur Fridays. In December 2022, the city put up signs designating this street as the "Arenas District," as well as a sign that reads, "Drag Queen Crossing." When it opened in 1991, Streetbar was the first gay bar on Arenas Road and is still going strong. According to co-owner David Farnsworth, "We are like a gay community-center bar. Local gay men treat this as their living room."

PERSONAL NOTE: I am always surprised at how straights and gays mix so freely in the desert. After I bought my condo, I hired a handyman to install my TV and ceiling fans. Named Mike, he drove a pickup, wore a tool belt and was as straight as I-10 is from Palm Springs to Indio. When I said to him, "I wish I had your ability to install and fix things," he replied matter-of-factly, "Then you need to find a husband who can."

- Arenas District -

✳ GAY PRIDE

Most gay pride parades take place in June, which coincides with the June 28-July 3, 1969 Stonewall riots in New York City. Because of summer temperatures here, the parade takes place on the first weekend in November. It's an all-inclusive event: high school bands, firemen, health workers, drag queens, city employees, pets all join in to show their support of gay rights and culture. At left Sadie Ladie, AKA Ryan Sihapanya-Allen.

FUN FACT

Palm Springs reportedly has the highest percentage of LGBTQ people than any other city in the country. Estimates say that between 40% and 55% of the city is LGBTQ. This glamorous desert getaway achieved a measure of fame in 2019 when voters elected the nation's first city council consisting entirely of LGBTQ members. Controversy surrounded one female councilmember who came out as bisexual during her election campaign. Some say she said that to get votes.

What to SEE in Palm Springs

15

Backstreet Art District

2600 Cherokee Way, South Palm Springs

Resembling a strip mall, the Backstreet Art District is across from a car dealership and a mobile home park. This is not the kind of place you go for a Sonny & Cher souvenir coffee mug. You'll find instead innovative art works in various media created by local artists.

- Backstreet Art District -

Bank of America
588 South Palm Canyon Drive, Financial District

The earth-toned, blue mosaic Bank of America was built in 1969 and was considered at the time to be the most beautiful building in Palm Springs. Maybe it still is. No two of its curved sides are the same; and because of its triangular lot, all four sides are easily visible from South Palm Canyon and Indian Canyon drives. The architect was Rudy Baumfield, who designed the Southdale Center in Edina, Minn., the country's first indoor shopping mall. Baumfield modeled the bank after Swiss-French architect Le Corbusier's art nouveau Chapel of Notre-Dame-du-Haut in Ronchamp, France. Gene Autry, who did his banking here, proposed to and married its manager, Jackie Ellam, in 1981. At the time, Autry had just sold his radio stations in Los Angeles for hundreds of millions. He bought her the Gene Autry mansion in Old Las Palmas.

PERSONAL NOTE: I was giving a tour to an elderly French couple when the Bank of America came into view. "Arretez la voiture," the husband said to me. "I know that building, my uncle is a priest at the Notre-Dame-du-Haut." Using his iPhone he took photos of the bank from every angle and sent them off to him.

- Bank of America -

Barry Manilow's Cliffside Estate

2196 South Camino Barranca, The Mesa

I always ask visitors if they are Barry Manilow fans. I either get a definitive yes or no. If I get a yes, which I usually do, I show them Barry Manilow's cliffside Spanish revivalist estate in The Mesa neighborhood, where he lives year-round. It was built in 1935 and has eight bedrooms, six bathrooms and almost 10,000 square-feet of living space. I remember a 50-something-year-old "Fanilow" who became so overheated at seeing his villa that she jumped out of my van and ran toward it — threatening to scale the cliff and throw her underwear over his stone wall.

Barry's villa can best be seen from West Camino Descanso, a narrow road that heads west off South Palm Canyon Drive. Where the road curves south, do a U-turn in your car to see it. The view used to be better until a ficus tree hedge was planted on the left side of the street.

FUN FACT

Almost every year, Manilow does a five-night concert stand at the McCallum Theater in Palm Desert and donates the proceeds to Coachella Valley non-profits.

- Barry Manilow's Cliffside Estate -

Bing Crosby's House
1011 El Alameda, Movie Colony East

When giving tours, I ask people who holds the record for the world's best-selling single. Almost everyone says Elvis Presley, with Michael Jackson a close second. It was, however, crooner Bing Crosby. His rendition of Irving Berlin's "White Christmas" has sold more than 50 million copies. Crosby lived in this three-bedroom, three-bathroom house with his first wife, Dixie, and their twin sons for 30 years, well into the 1960s, which is when he built a compound in Rancho Mirage near Frank Sinatra's. It was in that compound, not this house, that JFK rendezvoused with Marilyn Monroe. Built in 1934, this casa is considered a shining example of California's vanishing Spanish Mission ranch-style architecture. As for crooners, they are a vanishing breed too.

FACT CHECKING: Local myth says that Dorothy Lamour resided at 1029 East Alameda, which is next door to Bing's house. The story goes that the two houses were originally one and that Bing cut them in half so Dorothy, who starred with him and Bob Hope in "The Road to..." pictures could be his neighbor. There is no evidence that that the two houses were ever connected. Bing's was built in 1934 and Dorothy's so-called house was built the following year. In her auto autobiography, "My Side of the Road," Lamour never mentions Palm Springs.

FUN FACT

The last white Christmas we had in Palm Springs was on Jan. 1, 1979, when an inch and a half of snow fell.

- Bing Crosby's House -

Bob Hope's First House
1014 East Buena Vista Drive, Movie Colony East

Bob Hope bought his first and somewhat modest house in Palm Springs in 1941. It's located just east of Ruth Hardy Park, at the busy, northeast corner of Avenida Caballeros and East Buena Vista Drive. It was built in 1936 and has three bedrooms and three bathrooms. The Hopes lived in it until 1946, which is when their fourth child came along and more space was needed. A plaque out front says Casa Hope. What superstar today would live so modestly?

FUN FACT

Hope never sold his first or second house. At the time of his death in 2003 his real estate holdings in an around Palm Springs were estimated to be $50,000,000. In 1968 he donated 80 acres of land in Rancho Mirage to   build the Eisenhower Medical Center.

- Bob Hope's First House -

Bob Hope's Second House
1188 East El Alameda, Movie Colony East

Bob Hope once boasted in a TV interview that he spent half the year in Palm Springs.

The plaque on the white brick wall reads "Home of Hope." Of his and Dolores' three houses in Palm Springs, this was their favorite, which they bought in 1946. Located in the Movie Colony East, it was built in 1935 and has five bedrooms and five bathrooms.. As is common in these parts, the swimming pool is in the front of the house and shielded by a ficus tree privacy hedge. Hope preferred this house to his enormous, futuristic third house at Southridge. From here he could walk to the village and was surrounded by friends like Bing Crosby, who was just up the street. The Hope estate owned it up until 2013, which is a year after Dolores died. It's now a vacation rental.

Bob Hope's Southridge House

2466 Southridge Drive, South Palm Springs

Photograph by Bill Swindle

*When I take people on tours of Palm Springs, I like to start at Bob Hope's third house, as it combines celebrity, architecture, tragedy and triumph — everything that makes Palm Springs what it is. Even if someone doesn't know who Bob Hope was, the house stands alone as its own story. When I asked modernist **architect Hugh Kaptur** his opinion of it, he said, "This is not a house. It's a monument."*

With its triangular, undulating roof, Bob Hope's house, located in the gated Southridge neighborhood overlooking Palm Springs, is the most visible abode in our city. The seven-bedroom, 10-bathroom, 23,600-square foot residence was designed by mid-century architect John Lautner, who catered to the very wealthy. He left the center of the roof open so that Bob could stargaze. The outdoor (not the indoor) swimming pool is shaped like the comic's ski nose. The dining room alone seats 300. Lautner said he wanted to build a house using natural materials that embraced the desert and that the desert embraced back. When Hope saw the plans for the house, he said, "If the Martians ever do land here, they'll know where to go."

The house has a history as rocky as its surroundings. As final touches were being put on it in 1973, a spark from a welder's torch burned it down in 15 minutes. Just as construction got restarted, the house's famed interior designer, Alfred Elrod, and his assistant were killed after the sports car they were riding in got hit in the early morning by a drunk 16-year-old male.

- Bob Hope's Southridge House -

Dolores Hope never liked the house, inside or out. Hugh Kaptur told me "She had a terrible relationship with John Lautner." Once Elrod was out of the picture, Dolores brought in an interior designer to carry out her vision of a Beverly Hills mansion: So long natural materials and minimalistic furniture. What emerged was a yellow-and-pink-themed palace with smoked mirrors everywhere. She had the copper roof covered in granite, then painted pink on the advice of her friend, Leonore Annenberg. Feeling hopeless, Lautner no longer claimed the house as his. He died in 1994.

The Hopes didn't spend a lot of time in this house. They mostly used it for social gatherings. The Coachella Valley event of the year was the annual mid-winter party Dolores would throw at the conclusion of the Bob Hope Classic. Despite it being catered, Dolores prepared the antipasto platter.

Aftermath of fire that destroyed Bob Hope's house (Photograph courtesy of the Palm Springs Historical Society - All Rights Reserved)

The house does, however, have a happy ending, even though Lautner didn't live to see it. After the Hopes died (Bob in 2003 at age 100; Dolores in 2011 at 102), the house was put on market for $50 million by their children. California supermarket magnate and investor Ron Burkle bought it for a

- Bob Hope's Southridge House -

reduced $13 million. A billionaire several times over, he likes to buy and restore historic houses. He was able to locate Lautner's assistant, an Argentinian woman named Helena Arahuete, to head the restoration project. Arahuete was in possession of Lautner's designs and blueprints. She spent three years at the Hope house redoing every aspect of it. As of 2019, the house and metal roof was exactly as Lautner envisioned it.

President Dwight Eisenhower and Bob Hope at the Bob Hope Desert Classic (Photos courtesy of the Palm Springs Historical Society All Rights Reserved)

Attention Young People: If you don't know who Bob Hope was, let me tell you: He was one of the most popular entertainers of the 20th century. His resume included comedian, movie star, TV and radio performer, entertainer of U.S. troops abroad, one-time pro boxer, golfer (the Bob Hope Desert Classic), philanthropist, and host to visiting dignitaries, including U.S. presidents. Like his Southridge house, he was quite visible in Palm Springs. He was often seen about town and attended church at Saint Theresa's on Ramon Road. He died at age 100 on July 27, 2003.

- Bob Hope's Southridge House -

BARGAIN BOB

Although Bob Hope was one of the wealthiest celebrities on the planet, he liked a bargain. Jim Mahoney, who was his publicist in the 1990s and who lives in La Quinta, shared an example of Hope's frugality when he spoke at Don Wardell's live, weekly radio show, "Martinis, Mimosas & Music" (107.3 Mod FM) at the Cascade Lounge of the Palm Springs Agua Caliente Casino. Mahoney recalled running into Hope at a fast food drive-through off Interstate 10, far from his house. Startled, Mahoney asked Hope what he was doing there. Hope reached into his pocket and pulled out a piece of paper. "Well," he said, "I've got these coupons." *(Mahoney was a publicist to many of Hollywood's greatest stars, starting with Clark Gable. In his memoir, "Get Mahoney!", he writes about his clients, many of whom, like Steve McQueen, Debbie Reynolds and Frank Sinatra, made Palm Springs their second home.')*

INSIDER'S TIP: Best view of the Hope house: Take East Palm Canyon Drive heading south and turn right on Cherokee Way. Proceed down the road, stopping before a mobile home park (don't drive through it, though; the owner isn't very welcoming). Look up, and there it is. Even better, park in the Art District lot.

- Bob Hope's Southridge House -

Boxing Club

225 South El Cielo Road, Airport

Built in 1966, this pug-sized, mid-century building that's across the highway from the PS Airport was originally home to the Department of Motor Vehicles. At some point, it became the Boxing Club and is where professional pugilist Timothy Bradley, who's from Palm Springs, trained. No one knows who the architect was, though people speculate that it was desert modernist Albert Frey, especially since its round, metal sunscreen is like the one he designed for Palm Springs City Hall. Frey was far from knocked out by this building and denied having anything to do with it.

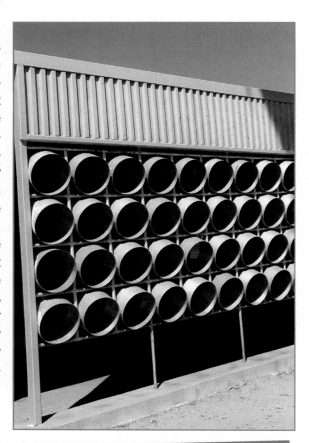

FUN FACT

Timothy Bradley competed from 2004 to 2016, holding multiple world championships in two weight classes, including the WBC light welterweight title. He and his wife, Monica, now own a chain of poke´ restaurants in Southern California, including Haus of Poke in downtown Palm Springs.

- Boxing Club -

Builders Supply
490 East Sunny Dunes Road, Vintage District

Builders Supply may not be as Instagram worthy as Forever Marilyn in Downtown Park. But it's historic — the oldest continuously operated business in Palm Springs. Builders Supply, now owned by Ace Hardware, is where the cognoscenti of contractors have been buying their supplies since 1926. It's located in the antique district, next to the Tool Shed, which is not a hardware store.

- Builders Supply -

Butterfly Roofs
Palm Springs

Butterfly roofs are as iconic to Palm Springs as pyramids are to Egypt. They didn't originate here, though. The roof was originally designed by Swiss architect Le Corbusier (see: Palm Springs City Hall) for a coastal vacation home in Chile. You can see butterfly roofs everywhere in Palm Springs: The V-shaped roofline was introduced here in the mid-1950s by architect William Krisel and the Alexander Construction Company with the development of the Twin Palms Estates neighborhood. The butterfly roofline proved so popular to buyers that the Krisel-Alexander team went on to create another dozen butterflied neighborhoods. Here, in the sun-drenched desert, the roofs proved a perfect fit. Houses topped with butterfly roofs seemed larger and more inviting. Because we only get five and a half inches of rain each year in the Coachella Valley, butterfly roofs needn't be concerned with water runoff. Krisel made the butterfly roof a trademark here and became its greatest ambassador.

- Butterfly Roofs -

Besides houses, you'll find butterfly roofs on all kinds of commercial establishments here, including storage facilities, fast-food drive-thrus, coffee shops. . .even Ralph's supermarket at Ramon Drive and Sunrise Way gives a shout out to the butterfly. Alpha Beta, the market that Ralph's replaced, was designed in 1960 by Alfred Frey, the Swiss-born father of desert modernism and a student of Le Corbusier. Alpha Beta was demolished in 2012. To help mollify preservationists, Ralph's incorporated the winged design into its roofline. It isn't obvious, but it's there.

- Butterfly Roofs -

What to SEE in Palm Springs

Caliente Tropics Resort
411 East Palm Canyon Drive, South Palm Springs

You don't want to anger the Polynesian tiki god standing in front of the Caliente Tropics Resort. Best to compliment him on his palm tree pompadour. The Palm Springs Historic Site board determined that the Caliente is the best remaining example of a Polynesian-themed motel in Southern California. It was built in 1964 and was originally called the Caliente Tropics Motor Lodge. Back then, it was forbidden to call motels in Palm Springs "motels." The Caliente was home to the Conga Room bar where the likes of Elvis Presley, the Rat Pack and mob figures would party. It's now the Reef Room, specializing in tropical cocktails and selling tiki mugs.

FUN FACT

Neighboring the Caliente Tropics Resort are renovated, mid-century motels that are popular with young people. The Ace Hotel, at 701 East Palm Canyon Drive, has monthly, full-moon drum circles. It also has a renovated diner called Kings Highway (previously a Sambo's) that has trivia and Bingo nights hosted by beloved local drag queen Bella da Ball.

- Caliente Tropics Resort -

Camp Curtis
641 North Camino Real, Movie Colony East

Located in the Movie Colony East is this sublime, Donald Wexler-designed house, which was bought brand new in 1960 by Hollywood golden couple Tony Curtis and Janet Leigh. The four-bedroom, four-bathroom house cost $46,000 and was dubbed "Camp Curtis." Jamie Lee Curtis lived here with her parents until their divorce in 1962. Leigh sold it two years later. The modernists loved to design houses that offered privacy in the front. Imagine gazing upon the San Jacinto Mountains as you float in your backyard pool.

PERSONAL NOTE: Camp Curtis taught me a valuable safety lesson when giving tours. I was on a packed tour bus, standing in the aisle facing everyone as I talked. As the bus approached Camp Curtis, a car came zooming through the intersection. To avoid a collision, Gary Ramey, the bus driver, slammed on the brakes, whereupon I fell backward, then rolled down the bus's metal steps to its front door. Shaken and bruised, I managed to get back up and continue talking. But from then on, I made sure to always hold on to a pole or the luggage rack.

- Camp Curtis -

Canyon View Estates

Canyon Corridor, Indian Canyons Neighborhood

This cul de sac is where the movie, "Don't Worry, Darling" was filmed.

There are two ways to get to Canyon View Estates in the Canyon Corridor. You can drive on South Palm Canyon Drive until you reach Avenida Granada, turn left and you're there. Or you can take South Camino Real through Indian Canyons until you reach Avenida Granada, turn right, then continue a few blocks.

During Modernism Week, tour buses make a beeline to Canyon View Estates, which consists of 180 condos designed by William Krisel and Dan Palmer and built by the Alexander Construction Company. The complex, on tribal land, was completed in 1965 after Krisel and Alexander had honed their modernism skills with Twin Palms Estates, Racquet Club Estates and Vista Las Palmas. Krisel designed Canyon View Estates with a groundbreaking vision.

Roy Fey, the developer who hired him, had in mind a typical, multistory condo building. "I immediately said I didn't think that was appropriate," Krisel recalled in a 2014 interview. "I thought phasing from single-family homes to condos should be a gradual step where it really was a single-story building with your own individual front door and your terrace and parking space, but there would be common recreational facilities such as swimming pools." Krisel envisioned common gardens, walkways and a putting green. "This was an era when people in Palm Springs owned individual houses with swimming pools and private yards," he said. "But there was becoming a need for people who weren't full-time residents to have a nice place to stay where they wouldn't have to worry about gardening and maintenance." The garden condo concept was born.

The two- and three-bedroom units (all have two bathrooms) are studies in modernism: clean lines, white exteriors, clerestory windows, atria, carports and customized breeze block walls. Each unit's master bath came with a tiled, sunken Roman tub, a must-have should Cleopatra come to stay. Telephone and electrical lines were buried underground. Canyon View Estates was designated a Gold Medallion neighborhood, meaning every condo was a state-of-the-art, all electric wonder. Condos also came with fashionable mid-century wood-grained Formica kitchen cabinets, wall-to-wall carpets and popcorn ceilings. *Still a mid-century purist?*

Billed as "The Ultimate in Carefree Living!", the 180-unit complex was built in stages from 1962 to 1966. Two-bedroom units (1,325-square feet) initially went for $22,500, three bedroom units (1,785-square feet) went for $25,000. As each group of condos was completed, a new homeowners association was formed. Although many of the condos here have concrete

- Canyon View Estates -

exteriors; others have natural stone. Fey insisted upon stone, thinking they looked more prestigious. Krisel, being a mid-century minimalist, objected but went along. Canyon View Estates was marketed to Mid-westerners and Easterners. Said the original sales brochure: "For those that enjoy carefree gracious living among gracious friends."

Driving along Sierra Madre Drive, between Avenida Granada and San Jose Road, is Azul Circle, a cul-de-sac that figures prominently during Modernism Week. It was used as a location for the Olivia Wilde/Harry Styles film, "Don't Worry, Darling," set in 1962. I watched some of the filming. Every street prop, including a garbage truck, trash cans, kiddie toys, lawn furniture and automobiles, were vintage. The complex has also hosted "Cul de Sac A Go-Go" parties during Modernism weeks, where "birds" in cages dance to groovy 1960's pop songs.

FUN FACT

Monty Hall of "Let's Make a Deal" lived in Canyon View Estates at 457 San Jose Road.

- Canyon View Estates -

Carmen Miranda's Cottage
1285 East Verbena Drive, Movie Colony East

Carmen Miranda (chica chica boom chic) was bigger-than-life, especially in Technicolor. So, it's hard to imagine the Brazilian bombshell ever residing in this cozy, 1,128-square foot house in the Movie Colony East. How could she have gotten through the front door in her platform shoes and tutti-frutti hats? I show this house on tours even if people have never heard of her because it's so modestly adorable. It was built in 1943 and has two bedrooms and two bathrooms. After selling the cottage in 1948, she moved into a larger house in the Deepwell neighborhood that isn't visible from the street (1044 South Calle Rolphe). Miranda died in 1955 at age 46 at her home in Beverly Hills. Her greatest performance was in Busby Berkeley's "The Gang's All Here," in which she sings, dances and even plays a banana xylophone in a colorful, phallic, surreal production number to end all production numbers. It's called "The Lady in the Tutti Frutti Hat" and can be seen on YouTube. In the number, Miranda sings that "It's OK to dress gay."

MIRANDA RITES

Tourist (and locals, too) can't believe a big Hollywood star would live in such a modest dwelling. According to J. Pierce, the current owner of the house, she certainly did live there in the mid-1940s, and he has documentation. "Sometimes I try to imagine Carmen Miranda's life here," he told me, "especially after a rainbow sunrise or an evening mountain sunset with a perfectly warm breeze. Whenever I need to de-stress, I treat myself to a Carmen Miranda day at the poolside and patio." *Chica boom!*

- Carmen Miranda's Cottage -

Cary Grant's Farmhouse
928 North Avenida Palmas, Movie Colony

The initials "C G" on the front gate of this rustic estate are those of Cary Grant. The suave movie actor bought the house in 1954 while married to his third wife, actress Betsy Drake. Built in 1927, the four-bedroom, seven-bathroom residence is called Las Palomas (Spanish for the "the doves") and is surrounded by several acres of gardens and trees. If the house looks shabby chic, it's intentional, as it's a replica of an Andalusian farmhouse. Wait a minute, Mr. Postman! Check out the mailbox on the gate, as it's a replica of the house. Grant loved Las Palomas so much that he hung onto it until 1972, three years after his divorce from Dyan Cannon. Grant, for a time, was listed in the Palm Springs phone book under his birth name, Archibald Leach. (I probably shouldn't reveal this, but you can get a sneaky peek of Grant's backyard and pool by looking though its back fence on North Via Miraleste, across from Ruth Hardy Park.)

- Cary Grant's Farmhouse -

✳ COPLEY'S
621 NORTH PALM CANYON DRIVE

When Cary Grant had company, he put them up at his guest house at 621 North Palm Canyon Drive. The residence is now Copley's, a restaurant serving upscale American cuisine. You can sit inside, though most diners prefer sitting outside on an overly large patio that has stunning views of the San Jacinto Mountains. Closed summers.

FUN FACT

In 1942, Cary Grant and his second wife, Woolworth heiress Barbara Hutton, honeymooned around the corner from Las Palomas, at 796 North Via Miraleste. Together they racked up 12 spouses. The press dubbed them "Cash & Cary."

FUN FACT

Grant, who died in 1986, was born in England, the son of a tailor's presser who went on to become Hollywood's gold standard of debonair. He once lamented, "Every man in the world wants to be Cary Grant, including me." Even though Grant had five wives, most biographers speculate that actor Randolph Scott was his true love.

- Cary Grant's Farmhouse -

Casa Adaire

417 West Hermosa Place, Old Las Palmas

Built in 1937, this 9,000 plus square-foot Andalusian hacienda is the Walter Kirschner Residence. It rubs elbows with Villa Paradiso, Old Las Palmas' grandest estate. Kirschner was the owner of a once-national chain of ladies' apparel shops called Grayson. He named the residence "Casa Adaire" after his daughter. The hacienda was meant to be a retreat for then-President Franklin D. Roosevelt and subsequent presidents. Kirschner was an early advocate of documentating the atrocities of the Holocaust and travelled to Europe with Gens. Eisenhower and Marshall to ensure these crimes wouldn't fade into history.

Sitting on three lots, Casa Adaire has eight bedrooms, eight and a half bathrooms, two guest houses and a lookout tower accessible by a spiral staircase off the living room. The house is classic Spanish Colonial Revivalist with its stucco walls, red tile roof and loggia-enclosed patios with water features, hand-painted decorative tiles and lush gardens.

Elizabeth Taylor and her third husband, movie and theatre producer Mike Todd, rented Casa Adaire in 1957 and 1958. Taylor celebrated her 26th birthday here. Among other gifts that day, Todd gave her a black mink stole.

FUN FACT

Called "Palm Springs, Here We Come," three episodes of "Mayberry, RFD" were filmed here in 1967. Tensions arose between Howard and Goober as they had to share a bedroom . . . like there weren't enough to go around?

- Casa Adaire -

Casa Cody

175 S. Cahuilla Road, Historic Tennis District

Casa Cody is the oldest working hotel in Palm Springs and is named for its founder, Harriet Dowie-Cody, a Vassar graduate and skilled horseback rider who, like Nellie Coffman, Ruth Hardy and Zaddie Bunker, was one of Palm Springs' strong-willed pioneering women. Harriet moved to Palm Springs from Hollywood in 1916 with her husband, William Bryant Cody, an aspiring architect. They came hoping the dry desert air would cure his tuberculosis. It didn't. He died in 1924. Needing money for her and her daughter to survive, Harriet opened a riding stable on the property. In 1932, she built Casa Cody, which consists of cozy guest houses. Casa Cody has the oldest performance stage in Palm Springs, built so that guests like Charlie Chaplin and opera singer Lawrence Tibbett could have a place to perform while staying there. The hotel property still contains some of John McCallum's* fruit trees and remnants of a stone irrigation ditch the Indians built to bring water to his orchard.

*McCallum was Palm Springs's first permanent white settler (see: McCallum Adobe).

- Casa Cody -

Charles Farrell Statue
North El Cielo Road and East Tahquitz Canyon Way, Airport

The dapper dan swinging a tennis racquet at the Palm Springs Airport exit is actor Charles Farrell, also known as "Mr. Palm Springs." The soft-spoken movie star with a Cape Cod accent had a starring role in the developing prosperity of Palm Springs in the 1930s through the 1960s. He and fellow actor Ralph Bellamy founded the legendary Palm Springs Racquet Club in 1934. Farrell was very active in village affairs. In 1948, he was elected to the city council and served as mayor for five years. He commuted from Palm Springs to Hollywood every week from 1952 to 1955 to play Gale Storm's father, Vern Albright, on "My Little Margie." Farrell was married once, to actress Virginia Valli, from 1931 until her death in 1968. They lived in the white, Spanish-style house at the southeast corner of Tamarisk Road and Avenida Caballeros, across from Ruth Hardy Park. He died in 1990 at age 89 and is buried in the Wellwood Cemetery, which is reserved for Palm Springs pioneers. The statue is by artist George Montgomery, also an actor and Dinah Shore's first husband.

FUN FACT

Farrell is credited with doing Hollywood's first male nude scene in the 1928 partial-talkie, "The River," in which he played "a naïve young man working on a logging camp beside a turbulent river." Too bad most of the film is lost; that could prove interesting.

- Charles Farrell Statue -

Chase Bank

499 South Palm Canyon Drive, Financial District

When you're looking at the Chase Bank at the corner of South Palm Canyon Drive and Ramon Road, you might want to stand on your head. That's because the bank's architect, modernist E. Stewart Williams, inverted the scooped arches that hold up the roof. Notice how they are reflected by a small pool with fountains. The bank, originally the Coachella Valley Savings & Loan No.2, opened in 1961. When Chase installed a bank machine on the unadorned façade, preservationists turned greener than a Federal Reserve note. In 2016, the bank was put on the National Register of Historic Places.

- Chase Bank -

Colonel Tom Parker's House
1166 Via Vespero North, New Las Palmas

If I know someone's a big Elvis Presley fan, I'll drive he or she, or them, by this spacious three-bedroom, three-bathroom house in Vista Las Palmas. It was owned in the 1970s by Elvis' manager, Colonel Tom Parker. It's been said that Elvis bought the house for the Colonel so he could be close to him while he was performing in Las Vegas. It's one of the 330 high-end Krisel-Alexander tract houses in the Vista Las Palmas neighborhood. The Colonel's backyard backs up to Dean Martin's backyard. Dean's late son, Ricci, told a reporter that his mom, Jeannie, used to peer through their backyard fence trying to get a glimpse of Elvis.

- Colonel Tom Parker House -

Cork'n Bottle Building

342 North Palm Canyon Drive, Downtown

OK, it's neither the Empire State Building nor the Chrysler Building, but it is Palm Springs's contribution to art deco architecture. Built in 1935, the Cork'n Bottle Building was originally occupied by the Simpson Radio & Frigidaire Company, which sold Philco, RCA and Zenith radio receivers. Good reception used to be a big problem here because of those pesky mountains. The structure was home to the Cork'n Bottle liquor store for almost 70 years. Coincidentally, the building looks like a liquor bottle. A plaque out front says, "The double and triple bands of horizontal 'streamline' moldings, flat unembellished blocky wall surfaces, and symmetrical façade are characteristic of the Art Modern Style." It has historical preservation status.

- Cork'n Bottle Building -

Cornelia White House
Village Green Heritage Center, 219 South Palm Canyon Drive

Located in the very heart of downtown is the Cornelia White House, one of the oldest surviving structures in Palm Springs. Built in 1893, it's made of recycled railroad ties. The house was originally part of the Palm Springs Hotel, the village's first hostelry and sanitarium, which was on North Indian Canyon Drive near the hot spring. It was owned by Dr. Wellwood Murray of Wellwood Library. Wellwood acquired the ties from a failed, narrow-gauge railroad line that was built to bring investors from the train station at the far north end of Indian Canyon Drive to a proposed housing and agriculture area called Palmdale at the south end of town. Palmdale never happened. Smoke Tree Ranch is there instead. Talk about surreal: Passengers rode through the cactus-studded, desert sands in two San Francisco cable cars whose destinations read, "Market Street" and "Sutter Street".

- Cornelia White House -

The White Sisters

There was nothing recycled about Cornelia and her sister, Florilla, two of Palm Springs visionary pioneering women. Florilla was a medical doctor and world explorer who had even visited the North Pole. Cornelia was a schoolteacher. Both came from a well-to-do family in Utica, N.Y. Cornelia was living in an American colony in Sinaloa, Mexico, when the Mexican Revolution broke out in 1910. Florilla came to her rescue. They, along with six others, escaped to the U.S. by securing a handcar and pumping their way north — next stop, Palm Springs! Cornelia and Florilla felt so at home in the desert that they lived here until the end of their lives. They dressed like cowboys and went on cattle drives. Before Welwood Murray died in 1914, they bought his hotel and lived in this little recycled house on the property.

The White sisters are shining examples of just how savvy and tough the women were who founded Palm Springs. Rudolph Valentino and his new bride, Natacha Rambova (née Winifred Kimball Shaughnessy from Salt Lake City), showed up at the Palm Springs Hotel in 1922 to spend the night. Both had just come from their wedding in Mexicali. The White sisters threw them an impromptu party to celebrate the event. When Rudolph and Natacha got back to his Hollywood home, he was arrested and jailed, which made headlines around the world. Because the Sheik of Araby had not been divorced from his first wife for a full year, he was charged with bigamy — by California law back then there had to be a year between marriages. Dr. Florilla White was called to testify that Rudy and Natacha had indeed spent the night at her hotel.

- Cornelia White House -

Dr. White wasn't having any of this scandalous nonsense. She admitted to the judge that the couple had indeed spent the night at her and her sister's little hostelry. However, she testified, Natacha wasn't feeling well so she slept inside the hotel while Rudy slept outside on the porch. That meant the marriage was never consummated so it wasn't a marriage. Based on Dr. White's testimony, Rudy was let out of jail and charges dropped. Up until Valentino's death in 1926 at age 31, Rudolph and Natacha loved coming to Palm Springs. When in town, they'd join the White sisters on Indian-led horseback rides through the canyons.

Dr. Florilla and her sister Cornelia White (Photograph courtesy of the Palm Springs Historical Society - All Rights Reserved)

- Cornelia White House -

What to SEE in Palm Springs

David H. Ready Palm Springs Dog Park
222 North Civic Drive, Airport

Is your dog k-fetching about too much sightseeing? Begging for a break? If so, you can bring your best friend to this free public dog park behind City Hall. While there, check out the intricate sculptural fencing by artist Phil Evans. He calls it Desert Reflections.

PERSONAL NOTE: One morning my senior shepherd and another dog got into a heated stand-off here. "I don't know what their issue is," I said to the young woman who owned the other dog. "We may never know," she replied. "Their hostilities could stem from a past life experience. Dogs have many reincarnations." I love Palm Springs.

- David H. Ready Palm Springs Dog Park -

David Lee Plaza Theater
128 South Palm Canyon Drive, Downtown

A Follies headdress.

Located smack-dab in the heart of Palm Springs is the David Lee Plaza Theater. This gigantic, 850-seat movie theater was built in 1936 as an adjunct of La Plaza shopping center. The opening movie was the world premiere of "Camille" with Greta Garbo, who showed up. True to form, she hid out in the balcony so as not to be seen. Other world movie premieres here included "West Side Story" and "The Music Man." During the 1940s radio stars like Bob Hope and Jack Benny broadcast from here. These national broadcasts helped cement Palm Springs' reputation as a celebrity playground. The Plaza Theater was home to the Fabulous Palm Springs Follies from 1990 to 2014. This was a Ziegfeld Follies-style dance and musical review with a twist: All the performers had to be 55 years or older — still daffodils by

Palm Springs standards. The ageless show girls wore headdresses, nude tights, and sequined costumes to perform their leg-splitting, razzle dazzle song and dance numbers. As for stamina, they did 10, three-hour shows a week. In 2023 the theater underwent extensive renovations and repurposing. Helping put a dent in the $16 million price tag was David Lee, who produced and cowrote such TV sitcoms as "The Jeffersons," "Wings" and "Frasier." He donated $4 million. City councils take notice when you give that much money. In June, 2023, our City Council voted to rename the theater the David Lee Plaza Theater. We still call it The Plaza.

Greta Garbo and Robert Taylor in "Camille"
(Photograph courtesy Palm Springs Historical Society - All Rights Reserved)

FUN FACT

One of the oldest and most beloved stars of the Fabulous Follies was Cheeta, a chimpanzee whose bloodline went back to other chimps who played Johnny Weissmuller's sidekick in the old "Tarzan" films of the '30s and '40s. Check out Cheeta's star in front of the theater on our Walk of Fame. Cheeta died in May, 2022, and was thought to be in his '60s or '70s. In his later years Cheeta became an artist. I got to know him and bought two of his acrylic abstracts.

- David Lee Plaza Theater -

Dean Martin's House
1123 North Via Monte Vista, New Las Palmas

Who could not love Dean Martin? (above). Palm Springs certainly did, from our nightclubs to our golf courses. He owned a four-bedroom, three bathroom Krisel-Alexander house in Vista Las Palmas (see: Las Palmas Old & New) He was its original owner. Dean left the house to his second wife, Jeanne, per their divorce agreement in 1973. Jeanne held onto the house until her death in 2016. Part of the Jeanne Martin Family Trust, it was mysteriously neglected until the summer of 2022, when a construction fence was put up. The residence was a happy place where Dean's grandkids would sell lemonade out front and that Dean himself would greet sightseeing buses. But after he and Jeanne's oldest son, Dean Jr., died in an airplane accident just north of Palm Springs (see: Mount San Gorgonio), Dino deserted the desert and didn't come back. He died on Christmas Day, 1995, in Los Angeles.

FUN FACT

In 1964 Dean released "Everybody Loves Somebody Sometime." On the Billboard Top 100 chart of that year, it beat out The Beatles' "A Hard Day's Night," "Love Me Do," "Do You Want to Know a Secret?" and "I Saw Her Standing There".

- Dean Martin's House -

Del Marcos Hotel

225 West Baristo Road, Historic Tennis District

The angular, lopsided orange door that you see at the corner of Baristo and Belardo roads is the entrance to the Del Marcos Hotel. Built in 1947, the Del Marcos was Palm Springs's first motel. But don't call it a motel. When motels were first built in Palm Springs, they had to be called by another name. The Del Marcos was the first desert solo commission for William F. Cody, who was part of the core group of desert modernist architects who arrived during the postwar period. Upon completion, the Del Marcos won an award from the American Institute of Architects as an example of new resort architecture. It's been described as "the quintessential Californian dream transformed into an accessible experience."

In 2012, the hotel was fully restored and won awards again for its audacious, populist take on modernity. Its 17 rooms feature mid-century décor and furniture. The Del Marcos was the springboard that launched Cody into the big time. He went on to design the desert's first country club subdivisions, including Thunderbird, Tamarisk and El Dorado. Cody, who died in 1978 at the age of 62, was the architect of St. Theresa's Church, his masterwork (see: Saint Theresa).

- Del Marcos Hotel -

Demuth Park
4365 Mesquite Avenue, Southeast Palm Springs

This spacious 61-acre park is our city's largest greenbelt. Located in the Demuth Park neighborhood of southeast Palm Springs, it has everything a park could offer: community center, fitness facility, picnic tables, baseball diamonds, dog park, tennis and pickleball courts and swim center. Great place to park your car if you want to take a walk, hike or ride a bicycle along the Palm Canyon Wash levee. Go west. Go east. It's all good. The Demuth Park neighborhood was developed after World War II as affordable housing for returning veterans. There are some cool mid-centuries in this tract. You can't beat the mountainscape backdrop.

SIGHTSEEING TIP: These three spiraled metal sculptures by artist John Clement were once in separate downtown locations. They've since been united in Demuth Park. The yellow one is "Squeeze," the red one is "Butch" and the orange one is "Ithiel."

- Demuth Park -

Desert Boutique Apartment Houses
2500 East Palm Canyon Drive, South Palm Springs

Located on the corner of East Palm Canyon and Farrell drives is the Desert Boutique Apartment Houses, originally the Desert Flower apartment complex. You can't miss it. The units look like giant Monopoly houses, only that wasn't the architect's vision. "My design concept," post-World War II modernist **architect Hugh Kaptur** told me, "were tents pitched around a desert oasis. That's why I had the palm trees specifically placed in front of each unit to further the illusion. . . The second-floor front-deck areas were originally a beige mixture. Now they've been painted turquoise on the Farrell side and chartreuse on the Palm Canyon Drive side. I like the turquoise but not the chartreuse." The complex contains Kaptur's most practical traits, thick stucco walls and recessed glass windows and doors for insulation.

- Desert Boutique Apartment Houses -

Dinah Shore/Leonardo di Caprio Estate

432 North Hermosa Drive, Old Las Palmas

This sleek, one-story, six-bedroom, seven-bathroom house was designed for the late entertainer Dinah Shore. Built in 1964 it's considered mid-century architect Donald Wexler's masterwork. Leonardo di Caprio bought the estate in 2014 for more than $5 million. He's rarely in residence. The estate is mostly used by event staging companies.

Caricature by Patrick Kelly

FUN FACT

The Dinah is the world's largest lesbian festival. Established in 1992, the five-day event takes place in Palm Springs in the early fall. The Sapphic revelry attracts some 20,000 partying women. The Dinah is named after entertainer Dinah Shore, who wasn't gay. So why name a gay festival in her honor? According to the festival's founder, Mariah Hanson, "lesbians like to play golf." So did Shore, who excelled at the sport, which she took up at age 52. She was so passionate about the game that she became the spokesperson for women's golf. Shore was a natural athlete who played a mean game of tennis.

- Dinah Shore/Leonardo di Caprio Estate -

✳ DINAH SHORE BRIDGE
Southeast Palm Spring

When driving across the Dinah Shore Bridge (on Dinah Shore Drive) between Palm Springs and Cathedral City go slowly so you can see the mosaics, which most motorists miss. Ignore the BMW riding your tail. Built in 1997, the quarter- mile long bridge crosses over the expansive Whitewater River wash. Embedded in each of the bridge's 12 columns are mosaics that were created by members of the Student Creative Recycled Art Project (S.C.R.A.P.) at Agua Caliente Elementary School in Cathedral City. Its mission is to actively engage youth about caring for the environment by recycling junk into art. Dinah Shore was, however, a bridge before she was a bridge. In a career that spanned more than four decades, she brought together two worlds: entertainment and sports. She was a much-admired figure in the Coachella Valley, where she had estates in Palm Springs and Rancho Mirage.

- Dinah Shore/Leonardo di Caprio Estate -

Downtown Garage
235 South Indian Canyon Drive, Downtown

Why would any tour guide point out a parking garage? Because it's free to park anywhere in Palm Springs. And no parking meters, which means no meter maids. Most downtown streets do, however, have three-hour time limits. Notice the garage's white canopies, known as tensile shade structures, on the roof floor. They are the vision of local **architect James Cioffi**, who also put them at the The Saguaro Palm Springs and at Smoke Tree Commons. These white shades have come to help define the new look of Palm Springs. Says Cioffi, "They give elegant shade."

- Downtown Garage -

Downtown Park/Desert Inn
Historic Tennis District

At the very end of West Andreas Road is Downtown Park, which was opened on Oct. 21, 2021. The 1.5-acre park is bordered by the "Forever Marilyn" statue, a parking garage, the Palm Springs Art Museum and a graffiti park, which is scheduled to someday become the site of a hotel and condos. Downtown Park includes an amphitheater, picnic tables, benches, art installations, indigenous plants and groves of pristine palm trees. Add to that a geyser-spurting water feature whose inspiration was the flowing streams of Tahquitz and Andreas Canyons. Watch the giggling young-uns try to outsmart it. Kudos for this beautiful addition to downtown Palm Springs goes to Mark Rios, principal of the Los Angeles design firm RIOS.

- Downtown Park/Desert Inn -

✳ THE DESERT INN

The Desert Inn (Photograph courtesy Palm Springs Historical Society - All Rights Reserved)

Downtown Park is where Nellie Coffman (aka Mother Coffman) built her legendary Desert Inn. (At some point, Downtown Park will no doubt be named after her.) Begun in 1909 as a sanitarium with tents and ramadas, the Desert Inn evolved into a world-class resort for the rich and crème de la crème of Hollywood. It was America's first desert resort and put Palm Springs on the map. Over time, Coffman acquired more land until her property swelled to 35 acres, stretching from North Palm Canyon Drive (where The Block and the Kimpton Rowan Hotel are now) to the San Jacinto mountains. The inn had tennis courts, a swimming pool and retail stores. Guests stayed in Spanish revivalist adobe bungalows that had red tile roofs. Gourmet dinners were served in the dining room, which had a string quartet. According to George Robertson, Coffman's son, "It was such fun to see the movie people join in the square dances at the Desert Inn. There were sheiks, harem girls and cowboys, all dancing and munching on Desert Inn fried chicken."

Coffman let it be known that guests had to dress properly and display high morals ("clothing optional" wasn't an option, and "Forever Marilyn" would never have been allowed on her property). World War II war correspondent Ernie Pyle, who stayed at the Desert Inn on several occasions, wrote, "She started what was to become the

- Downtown Park/Desert Inn -

Mother Coffman flanked by her sons Owen (left) and George (right)
(Photograph courtesy Palm Springs Historical Society - All Rights Reserved)

whole, vast vogue of desert vacationing." Five years after Coffman's passing in 1950, her two sons, Owen and George, sold The Desert Inn to Marion Davies, William Randolph Hearst's mistress. Davies, who had a brilliant knack for real estate, sold The Desert Inn to developers, who razed it in 1967. In 1992, the western block of Palm Canyon Drive, just north of Tahquitz Canyon Way, became the Desert Fashion Plaza, a shopping mall situated on 13 acres of Mother Coffman's land. It boasted 65 retailers, including such luxury department stores as I. Magnin and Bullocks. Out of step with the out-let-store times, the Fashion Plaza closed in 1992. The property sat vacant for many years until the Fashion Plaza was demolished in 2012-14. Imagine the tourist mecca The historic Desert Inn could have been if it had been repurposed. Think of all the beautiful boutique shops and restaurants bringing in all that money. Oh, Mother! (See: Le Vallauris)

"Don't it always seem to go/ That you don't know what you've got 'til it's gone/ They paved paradise, put up a parking lot" - Joni Mitchell

- Downtown Park/Desert Inn -

Dr. Smith/Dr. Peppers Office
483 North Palm Canyon Drive, Uptown

As you're walking along the west side of North Palm Canyon Drive heading north you may find yourself doing a double take just before you reach Alejo Road. Tucked away amongst some of Palm Springs most high-end restaurants is an old Spanish cottage sporting white walls, red tile roof and shaded veranda. It was built in the 1920s as a private residence. But as the city grew, there was an increasing need for community services, especially along "Main Street," as Palm Canyon Drive was called back then. Dr. Smith converted the cozy residence into a doctor's office in the 1930s. After him, Dr. Peppers occupied the adobe building from 1940 to 1948. Coming upon it today in the trendy Uptown Design District is a bit jarring, like bumping into Aunt Bea at Splash Weekend (see: The Saguaro Palm Springs). The cottage is now an administration office for Tac/Quila, Farm and Clandestino restaurants.

- Dr. Smith/Dr. Peppers Office -

El Mirador Tower

1150 North Indian Canyon Drive, Midtown

The Byzantine lookout tower at the entrance to Desert Regional Hospital is one of Palm Springs's oldest landmarks, though — spoiler alert — it isn't the original tower. The original was part of the famed, luxurious El Mirador Hotel — Mirador meaning "lookout" in Spanish. When radio stars like Jack Benny, Groucho Marx, Amos & Andy and Milton Berle were in town, they would broadcast their shows from the tower.

El Mirador Hotel opened on New Year's Eve, 1928, at a cost of $750,000, a hefty sum back then, especially since Palm Springs had just one paved road. The 20-acre resort was built by Palm Springs pioneer P.T. Stevens, who was a real estate mogul and founder of the town's Whitewater Mutual Water Company, and fellow developer, Alvah Hicks. Boasting its own airport and nine-hole golf course, El Mirador was a grand hotel in every aspect. The El Mirador immediately attracted the biggest stars and executives in Hollywood. Photographed at the hotel playing tennis, archery, golfing, or just plotzing in its gardens, were the likes of Marlene Dietrich, Humphrey Bogart, Katharine Hepburn, Clark Gable and Greta Garbo. Tarzan himself, Johnny Weissmuller, could be seen swimming in its Olympic-size pool that had five diving boards. Ginger Rogers was an opening-day guest. A pre -TV Lucille Ball practically lived there. Seen too were the eclectic likes of Albert Einstein, Shirley Temple, Salvador Dali, H.G. Wells and JFK's father, Joseph Kennedy Sr., who it's been said met his mistress, Gloria Swanson, there. Unlike other prestigious Palm Springs hostelries, such as the Desert Inn and Ingleside Inn, El Mirador welcomed Jewish guests. Because a lot of Hollywood stars and executives were Jewish, it became their getaway.

It was largely the marketing savvy of Frank Bogert who roped in the Hollywood crowd. As publicist for the hotel, he photographed the stars who stayed there, then sent those images to newspapers around the world, establishing Palm Springs as a world-class winter playground. A showman himself, Bogert would entertain guests by riding a wooden bucking bronco that was on a cable over the hotel's swimming pool.

El Mirador Hotel did its patriotic duty from 1942 to 1952. The federal government bought the hotel and converted it into a 1,600-bed general

hospital for wounded troops returning from overseas. It was named after Brig. Gen. George Henry Torney, who served as U.S. surgeon general from 1909 to 1913. Prisoners of war, mostly Italian, were sent to Torney, too. But not for treatment. They were brought there to make up for a shortage of civilian employees. POWs were assigned to certain departments, such as laundry, the mess and ground crews. They resided at army barracks at the airport. The men wore blue prisoner of war uniforms marked "PW." At the barracks, they were fed Italian meals. El Mirador reopened as a hotel in 1952.

The El Mirador hotel as seen from its Olympic-size swimming pool. (Photograph courtesy of the Palm Springs Historical Society - All Rights Reserved)

Mobster, gambler, oilman and philanthropist Ray Ryan and a group of investors purchased the hotel in the 1950s. Upon restoring it to its former Spanish-Revivalist glory, the celebs came back. But not forever. Over time, it became a money-loser. In 1972, Desert Regional Hospital bought the resort and its 20 acres for $4 million. In 1989, just as its transformation from hotel

- El Mirador Tower -

to hospital was completed, a fire destroyed the entire structure. Up in flames went the lookout tower. The fire was blamed on vagrants who were living on the hospital's second floor. After discovering the original blueprints, **architect Chris Mills** was able to rebuild the tower in 1991.

Palm Springs still has its most famous landmark, illuminated at night.

FUN FACT

I asked Mills where he found the blueprints. "A relative of one of the hotel's architects came forward with them," he told me. "They were the original ink drawings on linen. The only original part of the tower that wasn't destroyed by the fire was the weather vane, which is still there."

UN-FUN FACT

On Oct. 18, 1977, Ray Ryan was killed after getting into his car after a gym workout in Evansville, Ind. Someone had connected a bomb to the ignition of his brand-new Lincoln Mark V coupe. The murder remains unsolved.

- El Mirador Tower -

Elvis Presley's Honeymoon Hideaway
1350 North Ladera Circle, New Las Palmas

Photopraph by Henry Lehn

This space-age one-of-a-kind looking house in Las Palmas is popularly known as the Honeymoon Hideaway. It's where Elvis and Priscilla Ann were living when they got married. They didn't own it. But leased it. When gossip columnist Rona Barrett broke the news that Elvis and Priscilla were going to elope to Las Vegas, Ladera Circle became packed with fans, reporters and photographers, all hoping to catch them leaving the house. Feeling all shook up, Elvis called Frank Sinatra, who knew a thing or two about the press and screaming fans. Old Blue Eyes told Mr. Blue Suede Shoes to sneak out the back door of the house. Bordering the backyard was a then empty lot that faced 1356 North Rose Avenue. Go there and wait were Sinatra's instructions. He arranged for a car and driver to pick up Elvis and Priscilla and drive them to the airport where a private jet awaited. Everyone was left outside the house wondering, "Where's Elvis?"

Even without Elvis and Priscilla's imprint, the 4600 square-foot, four bedroom, five bathroom house would be famous. It was designed in 1960 by architect William Krisel specifically for builder George Alexander's son, Robert Alexander. Krisel and the Alexanders were business partners who built 13 modernist neighborhoods in Palm Springs. Robert and his wife, Helene, were

- Elvis Presley's Honeymoon Hideaway -

Elvis and Priscilla caught eloping.

dubbed the king and queen of Palm Springs, celebrated for their taste and style. He drove a white Jaguar and she did fashion shoots for local publications. "She was a knockout, and he was charming. They were rock stars," says local **architect James Harlan**.

A celebration of circles, the house is constructed atop three hefty, round structural pods on different elevations. When you look directly at the front of the house, you're seeing the expansive, curved master bedroom, where it's been said Lisa Marie was conceived. Even the kitchen is oval-shaped with a rounded kitchen stovetop. "The house of the future," as Look magazine dubbed it. For decades this house was a neglected shell of itself that housed an Elvis Presley museum. It was bought for $5.65 million in October 22, 2022 by buyers who spent months restoring it back to its dazzling presence. Too bad that wasn't true of Elvis, too.

✳ TRAGIC END OF AN ERA

On Nov. 14, 1965, George Alexander and his wife, Mildred, along with their son, Robert, and his wife, Helene, were heading to Burbank for a party on a Lear Jet. They were accompanied by Richard Koret, a handbag manufacturer, and Peter Prescott, the 11-year-old son of Bob Prescott, the founder of the Flying Tiger Line. Eight minutes after takeoff from the Palm Springs Airport they encountered a violent rainstorm and crashed into Indio's Little Chocolate Mountains. There were no survivors. Among the dead were the two pilots. Robert and Helene's daughter, Jill, who was 11 at the time, didn't want to attend the party and stayed home in the round house of the future. Architect William Krisel, who was George and Robert's business partner, heard the news on the radio. "I put down my pencil. Everything was over," he later recalled. No Alexander houses would ever be built again.

- Elvis Presley's Honeymoon Hideaway -

Elvis Presley's Graceland West

845 West Chino Canyon Road, Little Tuscany Estates

Elvis owned this 5,000-square-foot house at 845 West Chino Canyon Drive in Little Tuscany Estates from 1972 until his death in 1977. Nicknamed Graceland West, the Spanish-style casa was where he spent three months of every year. He bought the house in 1970 for $105,000 from McDonald's founder Ray Kroc. Elvis' "Honeymoon Hideaway" in New Las Palmas gets far more attention as it's accessible by tour bus and is architecturally important. Albert Frey, the father of "desert modernism," designed this house in 1946 for the Jergens family of bathroom products fame. Elvis added the wing on the east side. In 2019 the house was listed for sale as a teardown. A buyer saved it from demolition at the last minute. The new owner is keeping the wing.

The home reportedly took on a boy's club persona after Elvis divorced Priscilla in 1972. It's said that he used to throw water balloons at visitors. Elvis lined the living room with acoustical tiles and recorded nine songs here, including "Are You Sincere?" and "I Miss You." Ken Parker, owner of a local TV shop, told the Desert Sun newspaper that twice he was called upon to deliver big screen TV sets to the house. Whenever Elvis saw Robert Goulet on TV, he would grab his gun and shoot out the screen, Parker said. After Elvis died, Priscilla sold the house to Frankie Valli of the Four Seasons.

SIGHTSEEING TIP: To see the expansive backside of Graceland West, see Little Tuscany Loop Estates Drive chapter.

- Elvis Presley's Graceland West -

Eva Gabor Interiors
190 East Palm Canyon Drive, South Palm Springs

The Gabor family (from left to right): Zsa Zsa, Jolie, Eva and Magda.
(Photograph courtesy Palm Springs Historical Society - All Rights Reserved)

You can't miss the modernist, orange metal sunscreen at 190 East Palm Canyon Drive — at the curve where South Palm Canyon Drive becomes East Palm Canyon Drive. The orange sunscreen is where, in 1969, Eva Gabor, the youngest of the Gabor sisters, opened Eva Gabor Interior Design. When not in Hooterville, the "Green Acres" star worked at this studio almost every day, as did her assistant, Bill Hamilton, George Hamilton's younger brother. When Eva opened her shop, she told the Desert Sun newspaper that her signature look was to include at least one beautiful antique piece of furniture to anchor a room. She felt that too much modern furniture can look gimmicky.

Long before the Kardashians, the Gabors — sisters Zsa Zsa, Eva, Magda and mother Jolie — were famous for being famous. They defined the post-World War II Hollywood-Palm Springs connection. When any one of these glamorous beauties walked into a room or nightclub lights got brighter and arpeggios played. They had lots of houses in Palm Springs. The Hungarian beauties also had a lot of husbands: 22 in total, equivalent to two football teams. Actor George Sanders, who won an Oscar for "All About Eve," was married at different times to Zsa Zsa and Magda. He committed suicide in 1972 while living in Spain, leaving a note saying he was bored with life. After having been married to two Gabors, the Spanish Inquisition could prove a yawner.

- Eva Gabor Interiors -

What to SEE in Palm Springs

Farmers' Market
Palm Springs Cultural Center and Palm Springs Pavilion, Midtown

When driving around Palm Springs on a Saturday morning, the happiest sign you'll see is "Farmers' Market Today." The Palm Springs Certified Farmers' Market is held in two locations throughout the year. The outdoor market takes place Saturdays in October to May, 8:30 a.m. to 1:30 p.m., in the parking area of the Palm Springs Cultural Center, 2300 East Baristo Road. The indoor market takes place Saturdays, June through September, 8 a.m. to 1 p.m., in the air-conditioned Pavilion, 401 South Pavilion Way, just off Amado Road in Sunrise Park. The outdoor and indoor locations are only two blocks apart.

- Farmers' Market -

Fire Station 4
1300 South Laverne Way, South Palm Springs

Sometimes it's a firehouse that needs rescuing. Fire Station 4 in South Palm Springs was renovated and made state-of-the art in 2019. Funds for the project became available after voters approved Measure J in November 2011. The measure approved a 1% sales tax increase to revitalize local community services. Awareness for the firehouse's preservation came about because it was beautifully and functionally conceived by mid-century **architect Hugh Kaptur,** whose works include the Triangle Inn and Kaptur Plaza. "A home is totally different than a community project," Kaptur told me. "Doing a home is more personal so you're dealing with a lot more factors. The city's only stipulation was to make the fire station look residential, as it's in a neighborhood. My influence for the project was Frank Lloyd Wright's work in Arizona."

Forever Marilyn

Belardo Road and Museum Way, Historic Tennis District

When you first encounter Marilyn Monroe flashing her megawatt smile in Downtown Park, you may think the Hollywood sex goddess stepped out of a 1950s sci-fi flick, where fallout from a nuclear test has transformed her into a colossal giant, though not one seeking revenge but love. Called "Forever Marilyn," this 26-foot-tall, 24,000-pound statue was created by sculptor John Seward Johnson (1930-2020), grandson of Robert Wood Johnson, co-founder of Johnson & Johnson. It's his homage both to the actress and the post-World War II sexual revolution that she personified. The restored steel and aluminum statue was installed in this location in June 2021, with a million dollar price tag. It was inspired by Hugo Bernard's iconic photograph of Monroe from the 1955 movie "The Seven Year Itch," in which her skirt is blown in the air as she stands over a New York City subway grate. The statue was in Palm Springs before, from 2012 to 2014, on Palm Canyon Drive in the center of downtown. From there, Marilyn went on tour to New Jersey, Connecticut and Australia. Not everyone welcomed her return. Protests were held at the statue's unveiling. Some objected to its price tag. Some felt it was sexism run amok. Some were outraged at the closing of Museum Way to traffic. Others were offended that Marilyn appears to be mooning the Palm Springs Art Museum.

What does Ms. Monroe have to do with Palm Springs that affords her such a prominent place amongst us? Palm Springs played a major role in establishing her career (see: Racquet Club).

- Forever Marilyn -

✳ THE MYSTERIES OF MARILYN

Tour buses have for decades been stopping in front of a Krisel-Alexander built house at 1326 North Rose Avenue in New Las Palmas, claiming it to have once been Monroe's residence, either as an owner or renter. She never stepped foot there, according to the original owners who once told the Desert Sun newspaper that the house was built in 1961, a year before her death. How the myth of her living there got started they didn't know. All they knew is they wanted the gawkers, trespassers and occasional indoor intruder to go away.

Alfred Frey, the late father of desert modernism, claimed that JFK and MM used to hook up at his Monkey Tree Hotel at 2388 East Racquet Club Road, which he built in 1960. I've been on tour buses where the guides say that JFK and MM used to have secret flings at the Ocotillo Lodge, 1111 East Palm Canyon Drive. They supposedly had adjoining rooms that were connected by a secret door. There are no secret doors at the Ocotillo Lodge. I tell tourists that it isn't important whether Marilyn lived in Palm Springs or had a relationship with JFK here. The truth is we don't really know that much about her. What we do know is she had something even better, something that only the greatest of stars possess: mystery. That's why we still talk about her.

Loving cheers and angry protests at the Forever Marilyn unveiling.

- Forever Marilyn -

Frances Stevens Park

555 North Palm Canyon Drive, Uptown District

At the beginning of the Uptown Design District is Frances Stevens Park, named in honor of one of Palm Springs' strong pioneer women. Stevens earned a literature degree from the University of Chicago before moving to Colorado, where she met her husband, cattleman Prescott Thresher Stevens. Together, they drove cattle through the Rocky Mountains. They moved to Palm Springs in 1912 for her health; here, she began teaching and helped form our first school board. Prescott, who became a prosperous Palm Springs land developer, donated the grounds for the Frances S. Stevens School shortly after his wife's death in 1927. The old schoolhouse is home to the 206-seat Palm Canyon Theater, whose productions run from late September to May.

FUN FACT

"The Rainmaker" was born out of a 1988 decree from then-mayor Sonny Bono for public art. His administration formed Palm Springs's first public arts commission. It was thought that a fountain on the corner of Alejo Road and North Palm Canyon Drive would bring traffic to what was, at the time, an underused area.

- Frances Stevens Park -

The Rainmaker Fountain

This 35-foot-tall stainless steel sculpture at Frances Stevens Park was created by artist David Morris. It has four arms that bob up and down as they slowly fill with water, then tip and spill into a large basin. There's even a small amphitheater where you can watch the action and cool off in a misty breeze. The sculpture's colors were inspired by Greater Palm Springs (the blue of the sky, greens of the grasses, red of the terracotta tiles and burnt umber of rock formations).

- Frances Stevens Park -

Frank Sinatra's Twin Palms Pad
1145 East Via Colusa, Movie Colony East

If you read the historical plaque at the entrance to Frank Sinatra's Palm Springs residence in the Movie Colony East, you'll see that it says the house is called Twin Palms "for its historical trees" out front. What trees? The two big palm trees are there, only in the backyard. It wasn't always that way. The house was designed so that the front of it faced south onto Alejo Road. That entrance has a circular driveway that encompasses a flower bed — fitting for a star's arrival. No garage, though. Instead, an attached carport, typical of modernist houses. When the house was built the eastern end of the Movie Colony was mostly sand and Alejo a quiet dirt road. After Alejo became a busy, paved thoroughfare, there was a switcheroo. Quiet Via Colusa became the main entrance.

When the sun shines through the portico's sun lights, the pool's piano keys are formed.

Sinatra approached the young Palm Springs architect E. Stewart Williams in 1947 about building him a house. It was Sinatra who gave Williams his first residential commission. Williams would recall how Sinatra walked into his downtown office wearing a white suit and eating an ice cream cone and saying he wanted a Georgian-style mansion. Williams didn't think that was the right choice. Mustering his nerve, Williams told Sinatra that he should have a house that was "desert modern," thus more fitting the landscape and more reflective of his cool, swinging image. Had Sinatra insisted on the Georgian-style house, "that would have ended my career here," Williams said in reflection. One caveat about the job: Sinatra insisted the house had to be finished in a matter of months so he could celebrate Christmas there. Round the clock work got the job done.

- Frank Sinatra's Twin Palms Pad -

Frank and his first wife, Nancy Barbato, lived in the house for a year. After they divorced, Frank married Ava Gardner, and they lived there until Frank sold the place in 1954. (In 1957 Sinatra moved to his compound at Tamarisk Country Club in Rancho Mirage.) Notice the concrete privacy wall. It hides a grand-piano shaped swimming pool. Notice, too, the skylights in the roof of the covered walkway that leads past the pool and to the main house. When the sun shines on the roof of the walkway, per Williams' design, the play of light and shadow forms the keys of the piano.

This house was the stage for Frank and Ava's constant battles. In Gardner's autobiography, she talks about how one late night she and Frank drove to Indio on Highway 111, and upon arrival, pulled out revolvers and shot up the downtown (could alcohol have been involved?). An original bathroom sink still has a crack in the basin from a champagne bottle that Gardner allegedly hurled at her husband. Myth has it that she caught him naked in the pool with her close friend, Lana Turner. Some accounts say that it was Sinatra's third wife, Mia Farrow, who threw the champagne bottle. If so, she had a pretty good arm for a two-year-old. Farrow was Frank's third wife, 1966-1968.

Following Sinatra's divorce from Gardner he commissioned architect William Cody to build him a walled compound at the Tamarisk Country Club in Rancho Mirage. His Palm Springs modernist pad is now owned by a private corporation and is used for events.

PERSONAL NOTE: After I moved to Palm Springs, I quickly realized just how much Sinatra is revered here. A young car mechanic who was changing my oil had an image of the crooner's face tattooed on his forearm. I never met Sinatra, although in 1978, he announced to a sold-out house that he wanted to meet me. It started when I was assigned by my editor at the "San Francisco Examiner," where I worked, to review his opening night show at the Circle Star Theater in San Carlos, CA. I was blown away by his showmanship, at how gracefully he moved about the stage like a dancer. When I thought about it, he was a dancer, having made musicals with Gene Kelly. I went back to my office after the show and wrote my review for the first edition. The next night Sinatra stopped his band, turned up the houselights, reached in his pocket and read my review to the audience. "This man gets me," he said, "I want to shake his hand." Alas, that never happened. But what did happen is he sent me a large photo of himself that was taken at the concert. On the photo he wrote: "Thank you, John, for the kindest words I've read in many years, Affectionately, Frank Sinatra." Upon moving to Palm Springs, I had it framed. It hangs in my living room. Consider it my tattoo.

- Frank Sinatra's Twin Palms Pad -

detour

DESERT MEMORIAL PARK

Frank Sinatra's gravesite.

Francis Albert Sinatra died on May 14 1998 and is interned in Desert Memorial Park in Cathedral City, Section B-8, #151. To this day visitors to his gravesite leave him bottles of Jack Daniels and money to buy one for the road. Since his death, and up until summer, 2021, his grave marker read, "Beloved Husband and Father" and "The Best Is Yet to Come." A new one now says, "Sleep Warm, Poppa." "Beloved Husband" refers to Frank's fourth and last wife, Barbara Sinatra, who died in 2017 and is interned alongside him. It was no secret that Sinatra's daughters Nancy and Tina didn't get along with Barbara. In 2021 an unnamed person had the new marker made and installed. Also buried alongside Old Blue Eyes is his composer-pal Jimmy Van Heusen and his mother Dolly.

Sonny Bono's buried at Desert Memorial Park, too (gravesite B-35, #294). Other famous desert rats who chose Desert Memorial Park as their final resting place include director Busby ("The Gangs All Here") Berkeley, architect Donald Wexler, Magda Gabor, actors Betty Hutton, Cameron Mitchell and the "Thin Man's" William Powell.

To get to the cemetery take Ramon Road north until it hits Da Vall Drive. It's on the left-hand corner. Entrance is on Da Vall.

- Frank Sinatra's Twin Palms Pad -

SAINT LOUIS CATHOLIC CHURCH

Hello, Dolly!

The St. Louis Catholic Church in Cathedral City was Dolly Sinatra, Frank's mother's, place of worship. She was killed in 1977 shortly after the private jet she was on took off from Palm Springs Airport and crashed into Mount San Gorgonio. Although a private woman, Dolly's funeral was a worldwide media event, with news helicopters buzzing over the church. Fans jostled to get a look at the A-list of performers who attended. They included Cary Grant, Dean Martin, Danny Thomas and Red Skelton. The church is nicknamed "Dolly's Church" because of all the ring- a-ding-ding her son poured into the collection plate. His daughter, Nancy, had her second marriage there to choreographer Hugh Lambert in 1970. The steeple atop the church pays homage to the Eiffel Tower. It has to do with St. Louis, a 13th century king of France who was canonized in the Catholic Church, an honor no other French king received. Keeping the French theme, the church's 15 stained glass windows depict the Mysteries of the Rosary and were designed by the late, French stain-glass artist, Gabriel Loire.

DINING WHERE FRANK DINED

There aren't many restaurants and bars left from the days when Sinatra ruled Palm Springs. No Jilly's, Chi Chi Club, Don the Beachcomber, Doll House, or Bamboo Room. But there are a few hangouts left where he drank, ate, smoked and sometimes performed: Johnny Costa's Ristorante (440 South Palm Canyon Drive); Melvyn's Restaurant & Lounge at the Ingleside Inn (200 West Ramon Road); Riccio's Steak & Seafood (495 North Palm Canyon Drive); Purple Room (1900 East Palm Canyon Drive); Reef Room, formerly the Conga Room Bar, Caliente Tropics Resort (411 East Palm Canyon Drive) and Spencer's (701 West Baristo Road).

TIPS ON TIPPING: Frank Sinatra was known around Palm Springs as a big tipper. In his book, "Bedtime Stories of the Legendary Ingleside Inn," the late Mel Haber, who owned the establishment, talks about how generous Sinatra was to the waitstaff when he'd come for dinner, slipping $100 bills to the valet parkers. When giving tours, I like to tell that story hoping my passengers get the message.

- Frank Sinatra's Twin Palms Pad -

Franz Alexander Residence

1011 West Cielo Drive, Little Tuscany Estates

The Franz Alexander Residence was designed by modernist architect Walter S. White in 1956 and is on the National Register of Historic Places. Dr. Alexander was an internationally known psychiatrist who was a Berlin-trained devotee of Sigmund Freud. One of Dr. Alexander's clients was Oliver Freud, son of Sigmund. This 3,200 square-foot pad makes use of earthy, natural materials such as rocks, redwood and glass. The residence looks like a house where a progressive, mid-century shrink would live. Driving by it, you feel the urge to get out of your car, go upstairs, lie down on a Ludwig Mies van der Rohe leather sofa and be analyzed. Perched on a rocky ledge with V-shaped steel supports, it has a spacious deck that overlooks the Palm Springs grid. Check out the roof, which peels away from the structure. Roofs were a big thing with White. The doctor and the architect were a perfect match. While Alexander is noted for leading the movement looking for dynamic interrelation between mind and body, White focused on the dynamic interrelation between a house and its environment, *and how do you feel about that?*

✳ WHITE'S HOUSES

Walter S. White was a ground-breaking architect who did much of his work in Palm Desert in the 1950s, and who built at least 48 modernist houses there. He was noted for buildings with roofs that, according to University of California Santa Barbara's Architecture and Design Curator, Jocelyn Gibbs, "cause people to stop, stare and smile." His Miles Bates house in Palm Desert is famous for its curved roof that looks like an ocean wave floating unattached above the house. He died in 2002 at age 85.

- Franz Alexander House -

Frey House II
686 Palisades Drive, Historic Tennis District

Architect Albert Frey's small residence lurks above the Palm Springs Art Museum on Panorama Drive in the Historic Tennis District. It's a private street, so there's no getting too close to it. The best view of it is where South Tahquitz Drive meets West Arenas Road just past the Tennis Club. Frey House II was completed in 1964 and is where the "father of desert modernism" lived until his death in 1998. The interior of the 800-square-foot house is dramatically defined by a natural boulder that separates the living and bedroom areas. Perched part way up Mount San Jacinto, it's angled so that its view is straight down Tahquitz Canyon Way to the airport. Upon Frey's death in 1998, he left the house to the Museum, which offers tours during Modernism Week.

Tourist with boulder.

FUN FACT

Frey was a naturalist, so it's fitting his house was so private. There's a bell that guests rang to alert him before entering the residence.

- Frey House II -

detour

FORGOTTEN FREY HOUSE

Just off Highway 111 on the Palm Springs-Cathedral City border you can see a nondescript house with a yellow deck perched on a scrubby hillside behind the Glory to God Ministries church. This is the forgotten Cree House, built in 1955 by Alfred Frey for Raymond Cree, a wealthy realtor. Despite being only 1,300-square feet, it is anything but nondescript and no longer forgotten. The house was purchased in 1972 by the late Sherman Harris, who founded Sherman's Deli & Bakery in Palm Springs and Palm Desert. His son, Sam, who spent much of his childhood in the house, spent $1 million restoring it down to the smallest midcentury detail. He thankfully refurbished its grooviest feature: a three-panel hanging horizontal refrigerator-freezer. "Amazingly, no one ever replaced it," he told me. Frey liked to work with the latest building materials, such as the yellow corrugated fiberglass panels that enclose the deck and that you see from the highway.

- Frey House II -

Gene Autry Mansion
328 West Mountain View Place, Old Las Palmas

Gene Autry bought this 13,461 square-foot gated mansion in 1997 for his second wife, Jacqueline Autry (ne´e Jacqueline Ellam), who was 34 years younger than he. She was a bank officer who handled his funds at what is now the Bank of America on South Palm Canyon Drive. Autry died in 1998 at age 91, only a year after buying the 1927 estate for the two of them. Neither Gene nor Jackie had children. Jackie lived there by herself until 2020, when she sold it for $ 7 million. She used to joke that she didn't wear a medical alarm because if she ever fell and couldn't get up, no one could find her anyway. Notice the statue of a horse through the estate's front gate. This beautiful beast is a replica of Champion the Wonder Horse, with whom Autry made 79 western films.

- Gene Autry Mansion -

Gene Autry Plaza

Ramon Road and Gene Autry Trail, NE corner, East Palm Springs

Gene Autry, America's favorite singing cowboy, can be seen strumming his custom Martin D-45 guitar at Gene Autry Plaza, located at Palm Springs's busiest intersection. If you're hankering to get an up-close look at the statue by bronze master sculptor Delesprie of Los Angeles, park your car, horse or covered wagon behind Goody's restaurant and meander over. Autry, in his long career, made 93 films and was a fixture on TV and radio. He was also famous for his Christmas recordings of "Rudolph, The Red Nosed Reindeer," "Frosty the Snowman" and "Here Comes Santa Claus (Down Santa Claus Lane)." His theme song, which he's no doubt singing here, was "Back in the Saddle Again." That saddle was on his horse, Champion. An extremely savvy businessman, Autry owned radio stations, a TV station, and the Los Angeles Angels baseball team, which he brought to Palm Springs from Phoenix for spring training. At various times, Autry owned the Parker Hotel and the Ocotillo Lodge. When he died in 1998 at age 91, he was worth $500 million.

SITESEEING TIP: Just across Ramon Road from Gene Autry Plaza (northeast corner) is Red Echo, a 20-foot-high kinetic sculpture by Australian artist Konstantin Dimopoulos. It has flexible spines that move in the wind — and when being serenaded by Gene Autry.

- Gene Autry Plaza -

George Hamilton's Handprints
591 North Patencio Road, Cemetery District

I have given tours where no one has heard of Sonny Bono, Bob Hope, Dean Martin or Cary Grant. Yet when I say George Hamilton, most everyone, no matter their age, knows who he is. "He's the one with the suntan," they all say. That and some vampire films. It appears, however, that Grauman's Chinese Theater (now the TCL Chinese Theater) on the Hollywood Walk of Fame hadn't heard of him. That or they didn't think he was a big enough star to have his autograph and handprints in its cement plaza that contains some 200 other handprints, footprints, and autographs of Hollywood stars. Not to be deterred, Hamilton took matters into his own hands. On Dec. 7, 1967, he cast his autograph and handprints in the driveway of his hillside Moorish estate, where he no longer lives.

- George Hamilton's Handprints -

What to SEE in Palm Springs

Indian Canyons Golf Resort

1097 East Murray Canyon Drive, Indian Canyons

Opened in 1961, the northern course, which faces downtown, was the first 18-hole golf course in Palm Springs. The southern course, which borders the Palm Canyon Wash and looks towards Andreas Canyon, opened in 1963. If you're on East Murray Canyon Drive, you can't miss the two courses, as the highway slices right through them. Both courses are protected from the desert winds by the Santa Rosa and San Jacinto mountains. Of the six water hazards on the northern course, the most notable is the lake between the 9th and 18th holes that is home to the copper Walt Disney fountain, which to this day shoots water more than 100 feet into the air. You can sometimes see it as you drive along South Camino Real in the Indian

Scenic South Course.

Cahuilla artist Richard Salgado's Cahuilla Olla Waterfall (2004) is at the southern clubhouse Resort. "Olla" means basket in the Cahuilla language.

- Indian Canyons Golf Resort -

Walt Disney Fountain North Course

SITESEEING TIP You don't have to be a golfer to see the Walt Disney fountain up close. Just wander into the northside clubhouse, where it's clearly visible. Go earlier in the day, as sometimes it's turned off in the late afternoons. (The Indian Canyons house that Walt Disney owned until he died in 1966, and where his widow, Lillian, lived for several years afterward, is at 2688 South Camino Real.)

Canyons neighborhood. Disney, who owned several houses around the northern fairways, is credited with gifting it to the resort. It's been said, however, that the fountain was really donated by artist and set designer Harper Goff, who helped design Disneyland.

The golf resort cost $20 million to build and took years of complex negotiations with the Agua Caliente Band of Cahuilla Indians, who owned the land and still do. The courses were designed by William Bell, son of the legendary golf course designer William P. Bell. Architects Donald Wexler and Richard Harrison designed the clubhouse, which is on the north side of the highway and is a swinging example of mid-century design.

North Course modernist clubhouse

- Indian Canyons Golf Resort -

Indian Canyons Neighborhood

South La Verne Way and South Camino Real, Indian Canyons

The Palm Springs of your glossy, postcard dreams can be found in the Indian Canyons neighborhood, which consists solely of individual houses, condo communities and golf courses. Built mostly during the 1960s and into the 1980s, these custom-built residences were designed by such pioneering modernists as Stan Sackley, Hal Lacy and Dan Palmer. Houses here are as broad shouldered as Dynasty's Alexis Carrington. Their glass sliders open onto Bermuda blue swimming pools, lush green fairways and unobstructed mountain views. Front lawns look as if they had been cut and styled by Vidal Sassoon. I like to let my car get lost in Indian Canyons, exploring streets like Sierra, Yosemite and Alhambra, reveling in the sleek, minimalist architecture, brightly colored front doors, geometrically patterned breezeblock walls and Jetson-like atomic porch chandeliers. The future has arrived, yesterday.

- Indian Canyons Neighborhood -

You'll see meteor-sized boulders in front yards throughout the Indian Canyons Neighborhood. They represent the new look in waterless landscaping, which is called desertscape. Rocks and boulders are sold by the pound, so desertscape can be costly.

FUN FACT

The double-wide front doors of the 254 houses in the Canyon Estate condo development have oversized brass handles that were originally created to carry funeral caskets. The ungated complex can be accessed by taking South Toledo Avenue (heading south) and turning right onto East Canyon View Estates Drive.

- Indian Canyons Neighborhood -

✳ PINK DOOR

110 East Sierra Way
Indian Canyons Neighborhood

This house in Indian Canyons has an unexplainable, "Close Encounters" kind of pull, which has to do with its pink, monolithic front door. Over the last few years, thousands have shown up at all hours to be photographed in front of it. The owners bought the house with the door already painted that color. They have seen all forms of human beings invade their porch, walkway and lawn: Celebrants holding bouquets of balloons, women wearing ball gowns, men wearing ball gowns, screaming babies, rowdy infants, bridesmaids, gooey lovebirds, young women taking selfies as they do model poses in their trendy outfits, and more. Tour buses stop there. So many people have come to pay homage to the door that the frustrated owners have resorted to installing a sign in their front yard saying no to photographs and trespassing. I mean, they could just paint the door another color.

- Indian Canyons Neighborhood -

✳ BREEZEBLOCK

You'll see breezeblock all over Palm Springs, especially in the Indian Canyons Neighborhood. They're the patterned concrete blocks covering the sides of buildings and houses and are an important component of modernist design. More than just decorative, they offer shade and privacy. Breezeblock is in vogue again, evidence that good things do come back.

FUN FACT

Celebrities who lived in Indian Canyons include Don Adams of "Get Smart" at 2548 South Camino Real, Chuck Conners at 2585 South Camino Real, Monty Hall at 457 San Jose Road, David Janssen at 2220 Yosemite Drive, and Walt Disney at 2688 South Camino Real.

- Indian Canyons Neighborhood -

Ingleside Inn
200 West Ramon Road, Historic Tennis District

Behind the black iron gates at the northeast intersection of Belardo and Ramon roads is the celebrated Ingleside Inn. A heady breeze bears the essence of its former guests: Greta Garbo, Rudolph Valentino, Howard Hughes, Carole Lombard, Salvador Dali. The inn was built in 1924 as a private two-acre estate for Carrie Birge, the widow of the manufacturer of the Pierce-Arrow Motor Car Company. Each room was built with a fireplace and decorated with antiques that Birge would bring back from her excursions to Europe. Palm Springs pioneer, businesswoman and council member Ruth Hardy bought the estate in 1935 and converted it into a 20-room luxury hotel. She ran it with a Pierce-Arrow engine-like precision for 35 years. Hardy kept notecards on each guest, what they liked, didn't like; and discretion being key, who wasn't invited back. Some of those notecards are still at the inn. One says "NG" for no good.

Hardy owned the Ingleside Inn until her death in 1965. It was bought soon after by a wealthy San Franciscan, who after 10 years of losing money on it put it on the market. While the late New York businessman Mel Haber was vacationing in Palm Springs, he decided to buy the inn on a whim. He had already made his millions as the manufacturer of novelty items like dashboard hula dolls, rear-view-mirror dice and back bumper cat tails. Who better to take over the distinguished Ingleside Inn? Haber, as it turned out. He meticulously restored the hotel and grounds and added a first-class eponymous restaurant, Melvyn's.

The Ingleside Inn again became the place to be and be seen after Frank and Barbara Sinatra had their pre-wedding party there. In his book "Tales of the Ingleside Inn," Haber recalled denying entry to two "unwashed, hippie bikers," who he later found out were Steve McQueen and Ali McGraw. Nowadays, Coachella Festival stars like Taylor Swift stay there. So do artists and writers who, like Garbo, want to be alone. One of them is Palm Springs film director and screenwriter Ron Oliver, who checks in when he has a script to write. He posts Facebook photos of himself drinking martinis poolside, laptop in hand.

Film writer-director Ron Oliver poolside.

✳ MEL'S NOVELTY HOUSE

You've heard of "The Long, Long Trailer." Well, meet the long, long, house, one that might require calling Uber to get from one end to the other. Located at 700 West Stevens Road in New Las Palmas, this block-long residence was Melvin Haber's modernist house. Built in 1978, it's 13,305 square feet and has six bedrooms and eight bathrooms.

- Ingleside Inn -

Inspiration Point
Cemetery District

What looks like a stone fortress overlooking the O'Donnell Golf Club, at the far north end of the Historic Tennis District, is Inspiration Point, which is also called the Promontory and the Lookout. It was completed in 1939-40, courtesy of Thomas O'Donnell, the wealthy oil magnate for whom the golf course is named (see: Ojo del Desierto). During the Depression, O'Donnell conceived Inspiration Point as a make-work project to put local people to work. Men were paid $2.50 a day, which back then could feed a family. Carving into the granite hillside required picks, jackhammers and dynamite. The retaining wall was for decades the site of Easter sunrise services. While the pastor and choir were stationed above on the Promontory, the attendees were standing on the golf course, the women looking par excellence in their Easter bonnets. Today, the wall's only purpose is to be looked at and admired, like some people here. The road leading up to it alongside the Wellwood Cemetery is gated.

- Inspiration Point -

Invernada Estate
657 North Via Miralest, Movie Colony

Located in the heart of the Movie Colony is Invernada, which means "never winter" in Spanish. Designed in 1931 by portrait painter, muralist and draftsman William Charles Tanner (see: Ojo del Desierto and First Community Church) the 7,900-square-foot villa has six bedrooms and 11 bathrooms. It was purchased in 1946 by Tillie Lewis, a leader in the food packing industry — another one of Palm Springs' strong women who helped shape this town. Lewis changed hiring practices during the Great Depression by inviting people of all races, genders and faiths into her workforce. Invernada is one of Palm Springs's most elaborate examples of Spanish Revivalist architecture and has historic preservation status.

- Invernada Estate -

J.W. Robinson Co.

333 South Palm Canyon Drive, Downtown

Photograph by Lance Gerber.

The elevated glass building that you see at the corner of South Palm Canyon Drive and West Baristo Road was a winter branch of J.W. Robinson Co., an upscale Los Angeles department store. Built in 1957-58, the building's architects were Pierre Luckman and William Pereira, the latter a sci-fi aficionado who designed San Francisco's Transamerica Pyramid. Notice the building's cantilevered roof that imitates our mountain peaks and the cactus-shaped steel columns. Notice, too, how this building, like the Architecture and Design Center across the street, seems to be floating off the ground. It's dramatically elevated from the street level by four long horizontal concrete steps. When the sun hits the building's windows, it shimmers mirage-like. Imagine what stylish clothes were in those panoramic display windows. Famed posh Beverly Hills designer Alfred Elrod did the store's interior. People who lived in Palm Springs in the store's heyday say it was like entering a glass jewel box.

J.W. Robinson's is now home to Reforma and Impala, two Latin-themed bistros where you can eat, drink and dance.

- J.W. Robinson Co. -

The building, which got historic preservation status in 2012, was renovated in 2014 by **architect James Cioffi**. The most time-consuming, delicate task, Cioffi told me, was taking down and refinishing the diamond-shaped, white-gold tiles that line the side of the building.

✳ CIAO BELLA

A desert modernist, James Cioffi started his architectural firm here in 1978. Check out his 2014 energy-efficient twist on a 1960s condo complex that's located on East Tahquitz Canyon Way between Farrell Drive and North Sunrise Way. He named it Sophia Condos, "because," he told me, "Sophia Loren was the 1960s epitome of style and beauty."

- J.W. Robinson Co. -

Jack Benny's House

987 North Avenida Palos Verdes, Movie Colony

Around the corner from Cary Grant's rustic estate is a more contemporary house with a shiny brass "B" on the driveway gate. Jack Benny lived here in the 1950s with his wife, Mary. You can see more of the house by typing "Jack Drives to Palm Springs" on YouTube. This episode of TV's "The Jack Benny Program" aired March 11, 1956 and was partly shot here. Benny, accompanied by his sidekick, Rochester, and his parrot, Polly, come to Palm Springs for some much-needed R&R. The first thing he does upon arrival is to put on a bathing suit and take a flying leap off a diving board into his swimming pool. Only the pool has been drained. Benny spends the next four days in bed recovering.

PAR EXCELLENCE

After Jack Benny was refused membership at the Thunderbird Country Club in Rancho Mirage for being Jewish, pals Frank Sinatra, Ben Hogan, George Burns, Danny Kaye and the Marx Brothers, got together with other investors to build the Tamarisk Country Club. It was completed in 1952, a year after the Thunderbird – the Coachella Valley's first 18-hole-golf course — opened. The new club quickly became a legend as the Rat Pack's hedonist playground. Sinatra's compound, where he lived from 1957 until he sold it in 1995, was on the 17th fairway.

- Jack Benny's House -

Jack Benny's Second House
424 West Vista Chino, Little Tuscany

Jack Benny bought this seven-bedroom, six-bathroom house in 1965. It was one of the first residences in Palm Springs to have a lighted tennis court. You can't miss the house, which is on the northwest corner of West Vista Chino and North Via Norte. It's painted pink. Very pink.

FUN FACT

Part of Benny's schtick was his being extremely thrifty. A famous joke from a 1948 radio broadcast sums it up. A thief approaches him with a gun and says, "Your money or your life." Jack, the master of deadpan, doesn't say a word. Then the thief says, "Look, bud, I said your money or your life!" To which Jack replies, "I'm thinking!" (When Benny died in 1974 Bob Hope said: "For once, his timing was off.")

- Jack Benny's Second House -

James O. Jesse Mural

480 Tramview Road, Desert Highland Unity Center, North Palm Springs

In the summer of 1997, artist Richard Wyatt Jr. painted this stunning fresco that adorns the entire south side of the unity center, which is in the Desert Highland Gateway Estates neighborhood of North Palm Springs. The ten people depicted in the artwork are not supposed to be any real person, according to Wyatt. He told the Palm Springs Post that he wanted the mural to have a familial feeling, reflecting African Americans participating in everyday activities. Over the years, the desert sun has faded the mural's colors, and there's a movement to have it restored. Until then, don't think of it as faded but as having endured.

- James O. Jesse Mural -

Jerry Herman's House
444 Via Las Palmas West, Old Las Palmas.

The plaques out front of this 1981 gem tell you what famous person once lived here and who the architect was. The owner from 1999 to 2004 was Broadway composer Jerry Herman, as in "Hello, Dolly!" and "Mame" fame. The house was built in a boxy, "International Style" by architect Stan Sackley. As for flair, he put black marble balls atop the white concrete front fence. As for personal flair, he had a Jaguar collection and a curvaceous wife, Carol, who he'd photograph on diving boards in bikinis to advertise his properties. Until recently, Sackley, who died in 2001, had eluded the fame and praise of contemporaries like Donald Wexler and William Krisel. As this house, shows he loved shapely beauties.

Former home of
Composer and Lyricist

Jerry Herman

Architect:
Stan Sackley

- Jerry Herman's House -

Jungle Red
Ramon Road and Warm Sands Drive, Midtown

The residents of the Warm Sands neighborhood certainly have a warm spot for old movies and movie divas. In 2009, the city installed a red, 12-by-12 steel sculpture at the entrance to their neighborhood. The sculpture, which appears to be moving in and out of the ground, is a tribute to the color of fingernail polish that Joan Crawford wore in the 1939 film "The Women." In it, Crawford plays a conniving shop girl who steals away Norma Shearer's rich husband. After two years of separation, shy, demure Shearer finally decides to get her husband back. Her transformation from victim to avenger takes place the moment she applies Crawford's nail polish color to her own nails. "Look," she says, displaying them like a tigress, and in close-up, *"I've had two years to grow claws. . .jungle red!"*

- Jungle Red -

Seems not everybody is a classic movie fan or art aficionado. In 2015, the work by artist Delos Van Earl was nearly destroyed by a motorist who deliberately drove into it. News reports did not identify the driver by name or gender, just that the suspect was taken by police for a "mental health evaluation." As for happy endings: Shearer got her husband back, and Warm Sands got Jungle Red restored.

PERSONAL NOTE: Shortly after moving to Palm Springs, I found myself in the checkout line at Ralphs supermarket at Sunrise Way and Ramon Road. I had bought some watercress. The checker, Lee, picked the watercress off the conveyor belt and tossed it across the counter to the bagging area. "I'd rather eat a front lawn than watercress," he huffed. Seeing the startled look on my face, he said, "Don't you get it? That's what Joan Crawford said when Norma Shearer served her a watercress salad in 'The Women.' It's my favorite movie. I even own the script." Lee then told me about the Jungle Red sculpture that's in his neighborhood.

SPEAKING OF LEE, I've learned that one never knows in Palm Springs who a person really is, was or knows. Don't try name dropping here. When I was at Ralphs one day, I heard another checker ask Lee when his book was coming out. "So, you wrote a book?" I asked him, "about what?" "Oh, a celebrity I knew," he mumbled. Now I'm cynically thinking, Barbara Eden? Morgan Fairchild? Maybe he once did Connie Stevens hair? I nearly turned the color Jungle Red when Lee told me the celebrity was Freddie Mercury, his ex-roommate. The book is called "Freddie Mercury in New York: Don't Stop us Now!" and contains Lee's personal photographs.

MORE NAME DROPPING: I was giving a talk at an Assisted Living center here about being a tour guide. As I started to brag about having once gotten a personal letter and signed photograph from Frank Sinatra, a woman stood up in her walker and called out, "Are you talking about Frank Sinatra, my uncle?" "Your uncle?" I asked humbly. "Well, not really my uncle, but I thought of him that way growing up. His family and mine were very close. He used to babysit me." I didn't think she could top that, but she did. "If Frank wasn't home, my parents would take me over to John Wayne's house and he'd babysit me."

- Jungle Red -

What to SEE in Palm Springs

Kaptur Plaza

650 East Tahquitz Canyon Way, Midtown

One reason Kaptur Plaza looks so cool is that it is cool. Eminent Coachella Valley **architect Hugh Kaptur** designed the four-building site in 1970 with the desert heat in mind. Notice the breezeways, deep eaves, thick exteriors, recessed windows and other natural sun-deflecting features. Originally called Tahquitz Plaza, it received high architectural praise when it opened. Over the decades, it became a rundown shell of itself and in 2015 was scheduled to be demolished for condos. Just in the nick of time, Kaptur Plaza was deemed a Class 1 Historic Site, thereby saving it from the wrecking ball that was waiting off stage, twirling its villainous mustache. Kaptur himself was brought in to help with the site's restoration. In 2019, Kaptur Plaza received the highly prestigious Preservation Design Award for Restoration from the California Preservation Foundation. Since the late 1950s, Kaptur has designed hundreds of structures here, including residential homes, apartment complexes, civic buildings, commercial offices, fire stations and hotels.

"As an architect, you design for the client," Kaptur told me. "The client comes to you with criteria. Say the client wants two beds and two baths. I am going to come up with a piece of architecture and a floor plan that will satisfy their criteria but at the same time will be beyond what they imagined. That's my job, just don't tell me how to do it."

- Kaptur Plaza -

✳ PERFECT VISION

"I don't know what you call them," Hugh Kaptur told me when I asked him about these narrow, ovate windows at Kaptur Plaza. I'd heard them described as "eyebrow windows." "Never heard that," he said. What he did say is he differed from his modernist contemporaries when it came to designing windows. "I want mine to be beautiful. Not aluminum framed."

PERSONAL NOTE: Kaptur lives in a condo in the South Corridor section of Palm Springs. He redesigned its interior. I asked him about the kitchen, which is gorgeous. I was joyously taken aback when he said to me, "I got it at Ikea." He then added, "And I found the tile backsplash while wandering through Lowe's." Lesson reinforced: Good-taste is not about spending money but keeping things simple.

- Kaptur Plaza -

Kaufmann House

470 West Vista Chino, Little Tuscany

The Kaufmann House, designed by Austrian American architect Richard Neutra in 1946, is the essence of desert modernism. You'll know when you've arrived, as there's usually a small crowd in front taking photographs. The 3200 square-foot house was built as a winter getaway for Edgar Kaufmann, a Pittsburgh department store magnate. As for having great taste, he previously commissioned Frank Lloyd Wright to build his other getaway house, "Fallingwater," in southwest Pennsylvania. A 2001 New York Times article about Kaufmann contrasted the two masterworks: "Unlike Fallingwater, which sought to harmonize the man-made with nature, Neutra's sleek modern pavilion — floating planes of glass, steel and stone — stands in sharp contrast to the craggy hills. It is a pure and rational-looking alien on a snarled landscape." It's said that Wright was furious at not being hired to design the Kaufmann House. According to Palm Springs Life magazine, Kaufman felt that Neutra's angular steel and concrete structures heralded the future.

You can't see the back of the house from the street, which is how most admirers have come to know it. In 1970, photographer "Slim" Aarons took the iconic photo of its then owner, Nelda Linsk (right) entertaining her friends, including model and socialite Helen Dzo Dzo (left) (Wife of architect William Dzo Dzo

- Kaufmann House -

and later architect Hugh Kaptur) and actress Lita Baron (background), by the pool with the mountains as a backdrop. Called "Poolside Gossip," Aarons captured indoor-outdoor living at its dreamiest. The photo is now the iconic subject of postcards and wall posters. The house was used as Chris Pine's residence in the 2022 movie, "Don't Worry Darling."

Because of height limits, the house could only be one story. Neutra got around that by designing a roofed, open-air room with aluminum louvers that provide shelter from wind and sandstorms, and reached by an external stairway. After Kaufmann died in 1954, his estate sold the house. Various owners did updates, such as adding on rooms, altering floor plans and covering interior walls with floral wallpaper. Barry Manilow lived here for 10 years. When he put it on market in 1992, it was listed as a teardown due to all the "improvements." To the house's rescue came Bret and Beth Harris, a financial executive and architectural historian from Los Angeles, who paid $1.5 million for the house and spent five years restoring it. They were determined to go to any lengths to put the house back to its original look. Nothing was too minor. To replace the damaged stone on a wall in front of the house, the couple convinced a Utah quarry to reopen a closed section to get sandstone in the correct hue. In 2022, the Kaufmann House was put on the market and sold for $13.1 million.

Richard Neutra's mid-century masterpiece was a 13-room

UNFUN FACT

house at Tamarisk Golf Course in Rancho Mirage that he built in 1962 for Samuel and Luella Maslon, internationally known art collectors. After Luella died in 2002 (Samuel's death preceded hers), the modernist house was sold for $2.45 million to a mysterious contractor named Richard Rotenberg. According to the New York Times, "he walked into Rancho Mirage City Hall and applied for a demolition permit. It was issued that same day with no review and no questions, stamped and approved. Service with a smile. A week later the house was gone." Rotenberg never rebuilt and eventually sold the empty lot and left town. Neutra only built three houses in the Coachella Valley. Two are left.

- Kaufmann House -

Keely Smith's House
1055 East Paseo El Mirador, Movie Colony East

Keely's stone house looks as if it were built by jazz musicians.

Keely Smith

Jazz/pop vocalist Keely Smith ("That Old Black Magic") defined retro Palm Springs. A close friend of Frank Sinatra, her minimalist style fit perfectly in this mod haven. "She was the hippest doll in America, a real cool cat before they called it that," music critic Joel Selvin wrote. Smith lived here full time and was still performing in her later years, voice undiminished. From 1953 to 1961, Smith was married to singer, songwriter, bandleader and trumpeter Louis Prima. They are credited with creating the Las Vegas lounge act. Smith counterbalanced Prima's hyperkinetic presence by playing it straight, rarely changing expression. Cher says she copied her deadpan look from Smith, playing off Sonny just as Smith played off Prima. Smith bought this stony, three-bedroom, two-bathroom mid-century in 2006 and lived there until her death in 2017. Her swinging cover of Slim Gaillard's "Palm Springs Jump" made her synonymous with the town. *"You better get your luggage packed / Meet you by the railroad track / Shuckin' and jivin' swing / Everybody's jumping to Palm Springs."*

FUN FACT At Keely Smith's memorial service, Suzanne Somers recalled one of her favorite memories of Smith. Somers said that after 9/11 happened, she invited friends to gather at her hillside villa at The Mesa. Smith, she said, led the guests, who included Michael Feinstein, Robert Goulet, Merv Griffin and Jack Jones, in singing "God Bless America" in the courtyard. She followed it up with "That Old Black Magic."

- Keely Smith's House -

KFC
725 South Palm Canyon Drive, Vintage District

It's not always a craving for honey barbecue wings that has motorists braking as they pass the KFC on South Palm Canyon Drive. It's déjà vu. The Colonel's ghost must have gotten the message that Palm Springs is finger-lickin' serious about its architecture. The result: A fast-food outlet that could have been designed by Albert Frey, the father of desert modernism. In fact, the reason the building looks familiar is because it was inspired by the Visitor's Center at 2901 North Palm Canyon Drive, which Frey and Robson Chambers designed. Frey also did Palm Springs City Hall, which has a hole in the roof of its entranceway for palm trees, as does this KFC.

- KFC -

Kings Point

East Murray Canyon Drive & Kings Road West, Indian Canyons Neighborhood

Looking like a cubist version of a Greek island village, Kings Point is next door to the Indian Canyons Golf Resort's north course and across the street from the Indian Canyons south course on East Murray Canyon Drive. The 44 -unit enclave was designed by William Krisel after he completed the nearby Canyon View Estates. Developed in 1968-1970, Kings Point, with its white exterior walls, bold angles and clerestory windows, is his more luxurious take on garden condos. The development features much larger floor plans, four bedrooms, three bathrooms, double-wide front doors, no shared walls and two-car garages. Check out those painted front doors! The Kings Point Home-owner's Association notes that Krisel used an architectural style described as international moderne, which is characterized by boxlike constructions with little ornamentation.

- Kings Point -

Kocher-Samson Building
766 North Palm Canyon Drive, Uptown

If you're an impassioned devotee of modernist architecture, consider genuflecting when you pass the Kocher-Samson building in the Uptown District of downtown. Built in 1934, it's miraculously still here, though in need of restoration. "It is with this building that the legacy of Palm Springs' Desert Modern was born," says architectural design author Brad Dunning in the book, "The Desert Modernists: The Architects Who Envisioned Midcentury Modern Palm Springs" (for sale at the Architecture and Design Center, 300 South Palm Canyon Drive.) The Kocher-Samson was built by the very "Father of Desert Modernism," Swiss-born Albert Frey,

- Kocher-Samson Building -

whose angular, understated works include Palm Springs City Hall, the Palm Springs Aerial Tramway Valley Station and the Tramway Gas Station, which is now the stealth-winged Palm Springs Visitors Center. "Frey aspired to maintenance-free building that didn't need to be painted inside or out. He used concrete block, fiberglass, asbestos siding and aluminum windows," says Dunning. "His goal was timelessness both in materials and style, and he created a simple look that resists the winds of fickle fashion and is constructed in almost indestructible materials." The Kocher-Samson building was first used as offices for an insurance company and a real estate firm. Today, it houses a home furnishings store. In 2012 the Kocher-Samson was awarded Class 1 historical preservation status.

MODERN HISTORY

Modernism Week is an annual celebration of mid-century modern design, architecture, art, fashion and culture. It takes place for 10 days in February. A mini-Modernism Week is held in October. Modernism Week began in 2006 and attracts more than 105,000 participants from the U.S. and around the world. If you want to attend, go on-line and purchase tickets months in advance as most everything sells out.

PERSONAL NOTE: Not every visitor is enamored with our mid-century architecture. I gave a private tour to a retired couple from New Jersey who clearly weren't impressed. Finally, the wife blurted out: "What's wrong with people here? You don't like new stuff?"

- Kocher-Samson building -

Korakia Pensione
257 South Patencio Road, Historic Tennis District

Located in the Historic Tennis District, the exotic Korakia Pensione was once a 1920s Moroccan hideaway owned by painter Gordon Coutts, a Scot who had his studio there. It's said he built the palace for his bride because she refused to move with him to Tangiers. The 1930s screen star J. Carol Nash owned a Mediterranean villa next door. The two residencies have been combined into this alluring casbah.

"Midnight at the oasis/send your camel to bed."
— David Nichtern (performed by Maria Muldaur, 1974)

- Korakia Pensione -

La Plaza

100 Block of South Palm Canyon Drive, Downtown

This historic shopping mall is called La Plaza de California and is in the heart of Downtown Palm Springs, across from the Village Green Heritage Center. An open-air shopping mall, it can be entered on foot or by vehicle from either South Palm Canyon Drive or South Indian Canyon Drive. There is parking, but it is limited. Let's not call it a mall, though. La Plaza looks like a quaint Spanish village with its white, bougainvillea-draped walls, red-tiled roofs, courtyards, arched entry ways and landscaped gardens.

- La Plaza -

La Plaza is one of the first, if not the first, outdoor shopping centers in America. Opened in November 1936, it once boasted 36 shops, among them a drug store, grocery, beauty parlor, cleaners, clothing stores, a doctor's office and a Mobil gas station where, as you shopped, your chauffeur could get the Bentley washed and waxed. There was a subterranean garage for 140-plus cars, which is still there but not used. Tyler's Burgers was originally a gas station. Adding to its village feel were bungalows, penthouses, the La Plaza movie theater, and shopgirl quarters with fireplaces on the second level. The plaza's architect was Harry J. Williams, the father of famed mid-century architect E. Stewart Williams, who designed Frank Sinatra's house in the Movie Colony East. (Notice the generational split from traditionalist to futurist.) La Plaza cost $1 million. It had, and still has, a ground-level drinking fountain for dogs (pictured left). Alas, it no longer has water in it.

FUN FACT

Just how much of a village was Palm Springs in 1936? At La Plaza's opening ceremony, Nellie Coffman, who owned the Desert Inn, asked why the shopping center had been built in such a remote location.

- La Plaza -

Las Palmas, Old & New

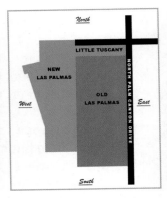

The Las Palmas neighborhood is bordered by Stevens Road on the north, Alejo Road on the south, North Palm Canyon Drive on the east and North Rose Avenue on the west.

I like to ask visitors, as I'm always asking myself: Would you, money no object, live in a Spanish-style hacienda or a minimalist mid-century? Red adobe or butterfly roof? Arched or clerestory windows? Lush or minimal landscaping? It's like choosing between Greta Garbo and Marilyn Monroe. The Las Palmas neighborhood is comprised of Old Las Palmas and New Las Palmas. In these two neighborhoods you'll find the very best of our two iconic architectural styles. Above left is a Spanish-style, Old Las Palmas entryway. On right a New Las Palmas modernist version.

Old Las Palmas is nearer to Palm Canyon Drive while New Las Palmas is closer to the San Jacinto Mountains. You'll find in Old Las Palmas Spanish villas sporting bougainvillea draped privacy walls. In New Las Palmas you'll see modernist houses that have low shrubbery and are on full view. The two neighborhoods are separated by a long street called North Via Monte Vista.

Old Las Palmas

Previously an orchard, the land was sub-divided in the 1920s by Palm Springs pioneer and master-carpenter Alvah Hicks. Some 300 estate-sized houses were built with over-sized lots. Streets were inspired by Fredrick Law Olm-

Typical Spanish revivalist mansion in Old Las Palmas.

stead. Hicks built his own Spanish-style adobe at the corner of West Alejo and North Belardo roads, which was bought in 1962 by Liberace. Hicks created custom estates on large lots that attracted the upper crust: Hollywood moguls, business tycoons, monied heiresses. Several of Palm Springs largest and most glamorous estates in Old Las Palmas are easily visible from the street (see: Casa Adaire, Villa Paradisio and Gene Autry Mansion).

New Las Palmas

Much of New Las Palmas consists of a 330-acre tract called Vista Las Palmas, which was developed by William Krisel and the Alexander Construction Company. Construction began in 1958. Vista Las Palmas was their next project after they built the highly successful Twin Palms Estates. Like Twin Palms Estates, every house in this tract development has a similar floor plan. Like Twin Palms Estates, most of the exteriors look very different from one another. An exception is the 19 Swiss Misses (see: Swiss Misses). Any mistakes Krisel and the Alexanders made in Twin Palms Estates they corrected here or improved on, adding maids' quarters, air conditioning, two-car garages and upping square footages to 2100. Utility lines were buried and no streetlamps to muffle the night sky. Original prices were around $40,000.

Mid-morning moon over mid-century modern.

Vintage Chrysler Imperial.

- Las Palmas -

SIGHTSEEING TIP: I rarely get visitors who aren't impressed by the Krisel-Alexander houses in Vista Las Palmas. I like to take those who are especially smitten on a short detour to show them my favorite row of them. They're located on Los Robles Drive, which runs parallel along the base of Mount San Jacinto and is only a block long (you can access it by driving west on Via Vadera). Each house is a jewel, my favorite being one named Casa Robles, which has an atomic porch chandelier.

This modernist Krisil-Alexander with a turned down roof was the model home for Vista View Estates (963 North Via Monte Vista). Vista Las Palmas is not a designated historical neighborhood. For that reason, the exteriors of many houses have been altered over the years.

FUN FACT

The largest concentration of celebs who lived in Palm Springs was in Las Palmas. As you drive around, you'll see plaques in front of houses that say who once lived there, including Kirk Douglas (515 West Via Lola), Mary Martin (365 Camino Norte West), Cyd Charisse and Tony Martin (697 West Camino Sur). Check out the colorful plaque in front of 275 Camino Norte West that says, "Only The Shadow Knows." This is where Bret Morrison, the voice of the mysterious radio-show crusader, lived until he died in 1974. You can find more than 600 stars' addresses in "The Best Guide Ever to Palm Springs Celebrity Homes " by local real estate broker Eric G. Meeks.

- Las Palmas -

✳ HOW DRY I

Dry Falls Canyon in the San Jacinto Mountains is direct
New Las Palmas. Notice the stone retaining wall that w
stop flooding if it ever went off the wagon.

Le Vallauris

385 West Tahquitz Canyon Way, Historic Tennis District

The only important legacy still standing from Nellie Coffman's Desert Inn is the Spanish revivalist house her son George Roberson built in 1927. George shared the house with his mother and half-brother, Earl Coffman. Roberson managed the Desert Inn, which was just across the street. He lived in this beautiful house for 50 years. Since 1974, it's been the high-end French restaurant Le Vallauris. In 2021, billionaire investor Ron Burkle, who bought and restored Bob Hope's Southridge house, purchased the restaurant and the Thomas O'Donnell House (see: Ojo del Desierto), the Willows Historic Palm Springs Inn and Colony 29, all in the Historic Tennis District (See: Downtown Park).

- Le Vallauris -

Lee R. Baxandall Bridge
North Indian Canyon Drive at Vista Chino, Uptown

Why is there a covered footbridge traversing North Indian Canyon Drive near Vista Chino? How in 2001 did the city council approve its half-million price tag? Why is it covered, and how come there are canvas panels along both sides? Why can't we see anybody walking on it? Why all these questions? Naked truth be told, the footbridge connects a clothing-optional condo complex called Desert Sun Resort (formerly Desert Shadows Resort) that is on both sides of North Indian Canyon Drive. Look for a big rock at the corner of North Indian Canyon Drive and Vista Chino that says "Desert Shadows... Enjoy Palm Springs Au Naturel." (Sadly, the rock was defaced in early 2023). A bridge was needed because the residents of Desert Sun said they didn't like having to don bathrobes to cross the busy four-lane highway. The official name of the span is the Lee R. Baxandall Bridge though locals call it the Bridge of Thighs. Baxandall was a 1960s Palm Springs artist, poet, nudist and founder of the Naturist Society here. He wrote "World Guide to Nude Beaches and Recreation." Baxandall lived long enough to be on hand for the bridge's dedication. When it opened, Jay Leno said he'd hate to be a toll collector on it, as the quarters must be pretty warm.

"Of all my works here, this is going to go down as the one most people know me by. I guess this will be my legacy," Palm Springs **architect Chris Mills**, who designed the bridge, told me. "I knew when I took this project, it would get a lot of attention. I had to solve the problem of making it functional and, because it's on city land, attractive. Did you know there are hooks under the bridge for the city to attach banners to? So far, I don't think they ever have."

- Lee R. Baxandall Bridge -

Liberace's The Cloisters
501 North Belardo Road, Cemetery District

Liberace had residences in Hollywood, Malibu and Las Vegas, in addition to Palm Springs. The Cloisters, at the corner of Alejo and North Belardo roads, was his favorite house. It's where he died in 1987 at age 67. When Liberace bought the house in 1962 it was a run-down hostel with 32 guest rooms that was scheduled for demolition. Liberace said it was crying to be saved and who better than the 911 of flair to do the job? Liberace said he loved nothing better than turning rundown estates into European-style mansions.

The 6,000-square foot house was constructed in 1926 as a private residence by and for Palm Springs developer Alvah Hicks, who also built the nearby Our Lady of the Solitude Church, where Liberace's memorial was held. The Hicks family lived in this house, then called Villa Theresa (named after Hicks' wife) until 1936. Hicks sold it to an owner who converted it to a bed and breakfast called "The Cloisters." Liberace furnished the villa in French Empire and Louis XV decor. In his vaulted-ceiling bedroom he had two canopied beds, one for him and the other for his beloved dogs. He hung crystal chandeliers in the mir-

- Liberace's The Cloisters -

Liberace, left, and his brother, George. (Photograph courtesy of the Palm Springs Historical Society - All Rights Reserved)

rored master bath and had holders mounted on the edge of the Jacuzzi for champagne bottles. (Go to You Tube and type in "Liberace in Palm Springs." He gives a tour.)

Despite Liberace's flamboyant presence, he was remembered by people here who knew him as quiet, dignified and generous. Upon his death flags in Palm Springs were lowered to half- mast. One man who grew up here told me that at Halloween he and his friends would always go trick-or-treating at The Cloisters: "Every other Halloween Liberace would open the front door and give out Hershey's chocolate bars. On the alternating years he'd hand out silver dollars."

detour

Pet Haven pet cemetery, 66330 Dillon Road, Desert Hot Springs. Six of Liberace's dogs, including Lady Di, are buried here. Their markers are signed, "Love, Lee."

Too bad Liberace didn't decorate this pet cemetery as it's pretty bleak.

- Liberace's The Cloisters -

Little Tuscany Estates Loop Drive

Little Tuscany Estates is tucked away in the rocky northwest corner of Palm Springs at the base of Mount San Jacinto. People who went to high school in Palm Springs say this is where they took their dates for an evening make-out session. I like to take people here because it's a whole different scene, a high-end, artsy grab bag of eclectic houses and estates on the rockiest of landscapes. Boulders to the left of you. Boulders to the right. You can take a loop drive on steep narrow roads through the area. From Little Tuscany Estates, you'll get great views of the Palm Springs grid and the windmills. As you tool along, don't miss the dry stack walls, which are stone walls that are constructed without mortar.

Dry stack walls

To take the loop drive: Head west on West Chino Canyon Road for a block or so. When it veers sharply to the right, continue along it up the hill. You'll pass Elvis's Graceland West house on the left. When you hit West Panorama Road, turn left and continue back down the hill. At the corner of West Panorama Road and West Cielo Drive is the Franz Alexander house that was built by

Willard S. White (see: Franz Alexander House). Heading down the hill on West Panorama Drive, look to your left and you'll see the expansive backside wing of Elvis's house.

The back of Graceland West.

Before the road veers to the left, you'll pass the George and Rosalie Hearst estate, a mini version of Hearst Castle. This is where Patty Hearst reportedly recuperated after her bank robbery trial. At the bottom of the hill is the Raymond Loewy residence. He was the prolific designer of the Studebaker Avanti, Coca-Cola bottle and Greyhound Scenicruiser, for starters. Desert modernist Alfred Frey designed his house in 1946. Its coolest feature is the outdoor swimming pool that extends into the living room. At one of Loewy's soirees, actor William Powell accidentally fell into the pool fully dressed. As any gracious host would do, Loewy jumped in, too, and summoned the bartenders to serve them drinks. Before you turn back onto West Vista Chino heading east, you'll pass on your left the Hollywood House, which was designed in 1966 by famed movie set designer James McNaughton. Be sure to wave to Jean Harlow as she walks out its large art deco front doors.

Hollywood House.

PERSONAL NOTE: My neighbor, Fred, who's a contractor, told me that he once remodeled Magda Gabor's house at 1090 West Cielo Drive in Little Tuscany Estates. "She wanted a bigger walk-in closet for her clothes," he told me. "So that's what I gave her. It's 1100 square feet with Laundromat monorails on the ceiling." Magda is buried at Desert Memorial Park in Cathedral City.

FUN FACT

Little Tuscany was developed in 1935. So named as the rocky hillside is reminiscent of northern Italy. Dry stack walls (AKA cyclopean masonry) is associated with Tuscany. Stones are placed on top of each other without the use of mortar and are held together by the weight of stone and the skills of the builders, of which there aren't many.

- Little Tuscany Estates Loop Drive -

Lucy Ricardo Bench

100 North Palm Canyon Drive, Downtown

The woman sitting on a bronze bench in the center of downtown Palm Springs — at the corner of Palm Canyon Drive and Tahquitz Way — is Lucy Ricardo from "I Love Lucy." Appropriately titled "Lucy Ricardo," the 1995 work is by Russian-American artists Emmanuil and Janet Snitkovsky, who are married and live here.

Lucille Ball had two hot loves in her life: Desi Arnaz and the desert. At the height of her fame in the 1950s and '60s, she split her time between Hollywood and the Coachella Valley. She wasn't a golfer, though. She preferred swimming, playing tennis, riding and smoking cigarettes.

Lucy was very much a part of the desert community. So was Desi, who she married in 1940 and divorced in 1960. She was crowned Queen of the Desert Circus Parade in 1964. Wearing a cowboy outfit, she waved to thousands of fans along South Palm Canyon Drive from the backseat of a Cadillac convertible. At night, she and Desi were frequently seen dining, dancing and doing impromptu comedy routines at the Chi Chi Club, El Mirador, the Racquet Club and other popular spots. The large stage at the Riviera Hotel (now Margaritaville Resort) accommodated the entire Desi Arnaz Orchestra. Lucy's phone number was even in the white pages of the phone book.

EMMANUIL AND JANET SNITKOVSKY
Russian-American
born 1933, 1934

Lucy Ricardo
from "I Love Lucy." 1995
bronze

Commissioned with funds
provided by
Walk of Stars, Liebling Trust and
City of Palm Springs
Public Arts Commission, 1995

- "Lucy Ricardo" Bench -

Cowboy Mayor Frank Bogert and Lucille Ball were such close friends that they called each other brother and sister. (Photograph courtesy of the Palm Springs Historical Society - All Rights Reserved)

Despite what some vacation rentals may advertise, Lucy and Desi never owned a house in Palm Springs, a fact confirmed by their daughter, Lucie Arnaz. It's thought that they may have rented the Samuel Goldwyn estate at 334 West Hermosa Place in Old Las Palmas while their house was being built at the Thunderbird Country Club in Rancho Mirage. A year after divorcing Desi, Lucy married nightclub comedian Gary Morton, who moved in with Lucy at the Thunderbird. Their union lasted 28 years until her death in 1989. Desi remarried in 1963 and bought a home in the Thunderbird communities. By all accounts, Lucy and Desi remained friends.

You can sit on the bench and get a photo with Lucy. You know you want to.

PERSONAL NOTE: There's a lot of speculation that Lucille Ball and Vivian Vance (aka Ethel Mertz) didn't get along when they did "I Love Lucy." I asked Vance about that when I interviewed her for the San Francisco Examiner. She told me that at first there was tension, but as time went on, she realized it was best "to hitch my wagon to Lucy's star." After that, she said, they remained close friends.

detour

INDIAN WELLS RESORT HOTEL
76-661 Highway 111, Indian Wells

Lucy and Desi decided to go into the hotel business in 1957. They bought 50 acres in the then undeveloped Indian Wells, where they built the Desi Arnaz Western Hills Hotel (now the Indian Wells Resort Hotel). If you're an "I Love Lucy" aficionado, the hotel has priceless photos of the couple on display.

- "Lucy Ricardo" Bench -

What to SEE in Palm Springs

Margaritaville Resort/Riviera

1600 North Indian Canyon Drive, Uptown

The resort's four-leaf-clover-shaped swimming pool.

The bow-shaped hotel at the corner of Vista Chino and Indian Canyon Drive is the epitome of 1960s glamour, desert-style. It still is, even though in 2020 it lost its original name, the Riviera Resort, which conjured up images of Mediterranean beaches, highballs, jet-setters and fin-tailed Cadillacs. Palm Springs's residents, by habit, still call it the Riviera even though it's now a Margaritaville Resort, a themed hotel that caters to the followers of the late Jimmy Buffet and a younger generation of vacationers.

Called the party-going, nerve center of the swinging '60s, the Riviera was a gathering spot for those who didn't need their last names to be identified, like Frank, Dean, Sammy, Marilyn, Rock and Elvis.

The Riviera was built in 1959 by the noted local hotelier Irwin Schuman who started the long-gone Chi Chi Club on South Palm Canyon Drive, which was the queen of Palm Springs's many nightspots. Schuman saw an opportuni-

- Margaritaville Resort/Riviera -

ty to build a hotel in this burgeoning resort town that could, like the hotels in Las Vegas, host conventions and business meetings. And so he purchased the 40-acre site from the Agua Caliente Tribe. The Riviera was Palm Springs's largest hotel for many years. In its commodious Riviera Room, big-draw entertainers like Liberace and the Desi Arnaz Orchestra often performed. The architect was Homer Rissman, who designed the hotel like a pinwheel. The swimming pool is located in the hub of the pinwheel and is shaped like a four-leaf clover.

SIGHTSEEING TIP: A hedge in front of the resort blocks its view. For a closer look, park your car on Vista Chino or in the Billy Reed parking lot. Then wander through the resort's main doors, which lead to the iconic pool.

Twisting the night away at the the former Riviera Hotel are the stars of "Palm Springs Weekend." (Left to right) Troy Donahue, Stefanie Powers, Robert Conrad and Connie Stevens.

FUN FACT

The 1963 teen flick, "Palm Springs Weekend," starring Troy Donahue and Connie Stevens, was filmed here.

- Margaritaville Resort/Riviera -

McCallum Adobe
221 South Palm Canyon Drive, Downtown

Located in the Village Green Heritage Center in the very heart of town, across from LULU California Bistro, is the McCallum Adobe, Palm Springs's oldest building. The Agua Caliente Tribe of the Cahuilla Indians constructed the house in 1884 out of adobe bricks for John Guthrie McCallum, Palm Springs's first permanent white setter. Originally

Here's where the first white settlers lived.

located on what is now West Tahquitz Canyon Way between West Belardo Road and South Palm Canyon Drive, the house was carefully deconstructed and moved to this nearby site during the early 1950s. McCallum's daughter, Pearl McCallum McManus, donated this land to the city with the condition that the McCallum Adobe, where she partly grew up and lived in as an adult, be preserved on it. The L-shaped house now houses the Palm Springs Historical Society, where you can see period memorabilia, photographs and short films. It also offers free walking tours (though be sure to tip your guide). You can see on the brick exterior wall of the house where the original Agua Caliente workmen inscribed their names. In gratitude, McCallum named many of the streets in Palm Springs after them, including Alejo, Amado, Arenas, Baristo and Saturmino roads and Vista Chino.

John Guthrie McCallum is the most important of all the Palm Springs non-indigenous pioneers and settlers. He was a self-taught man: attorney, newspaper editor and politician. He was so learned that people called him Judge even though he wasn't one. Name dropping? He knew Abraham Lincoln. His daughter, Pearl, said he attended Lincoln's inaugural ball and was at Ford's Theatre the night he was assassinated.

John McCallum

Pearl McCallum

(Photograph courtesy of the Palm Springs Historical Society - All Rights Reserved)

- McCallum Adobe -

McCallum first visited the Sonoran Desert in his role as Indian agent to the indigenous Mission Indians of Southern California. At age 57, he relocated his family and five children here, hoping the warm, dry air and spa waters would cure his son, Johnny, of tuberculosis. According to Pearl, the only neighbors and friends they had for the first few years were about 76 Cahuilla Indians. Mc-Callum envisioned Palm Valley, his original name for Palm Springs, as being an agricultural paradise. A year after settling here, McCallum began buying up large tracts of land from the Southern Pacific Railroad for as little as $2.50 an acre. Within three years, he had acquired 1,767 acres that would become some of the most valuable real estate in America — but not until decades after his death. McCallum, with the aid of tribe members, began plowing and planting some of the land he had purchased at the foot of the San Jacinto Mountains. He employed the Agua Caliente to build a 19-mile, stone-lined flume that carried water from the Whitewater River north of Palm Springs to his 80-acre farm, where he was growing oranges, apricots and grapes.

McCallum's dream of a desert paradise looked to be really happening. But over time, the farmers and homesteaders who moved here began leaving the desert with its intense summers and water fees. Son John's tuberculosis had been cured, or so it seemed. After seven years, it reoccurred and in 1891 at age 29, he succumbed to it. While McCallum was in mourning, Mother Nature really laid it on him: Three days of torrential rains washed away his orchards. The rains were followed by an 11-year drought that turned paradise into a no-man's land. McCallum died a year later, a broken man.

His vision of a thriving desert did not die with him. Pearl devoted her life to making it a reality. After her mother's death in 1914, she acquired between 5,000 and 6,000 acres of what is now Palm Springs. Pearl was a philanthropist whose numerous contributions included donating the land at the Living Desert in Palm Desert and funding the building of the McCallum Theatre in Palm Desert. By selling off land over the rest of her life, she had immense power over the valley's growth and development. She was loved and feared. Artist Gordon Coutts's portrait of her hangs in the McCallum Adobe. Although Pearl's wearing a frilly dress, she was more at home in riding gear. A skilled equestrian, her happiest memories were of riding horseback through the desert scrub.

- McCallum Adobe -

McCormick's Auto Showroom
244 North Indian Canyon Drive, Midtown

Photograph by Christopher Cole.

Attention vintage car aficionados: Day-to-day, you never know what makes and styles you're going to see in the picture windows of McCormick's Auto Showroom at the corner of North Indian Canyon Drive and Amado Road. There are often cars on the outside of the building, too. You might be old enough to remember when cars were glamorously accessorized, sporting white walls, chrome bumpers, hood emblems and shiny two-tone paint jobs. Pictured above is a 1955 Pontiac Chieftain just waiting to be driven home. It comes with an ignition key.

PERSONAL NOTE: I loved those beautiful vintage cars as a kid, though they weren't vintage; they were brand new. When the new models came out in the fall, I would make my father take me to the Lincoln dealership in Whittier, Calif., to look at the sleek, shiny new arrivals. I once told him I wanted the salmon-colored Lincoln Continental convertible in the showroom window. "Someday," he said, "when you have $3,000."

- McCormick's Auto Showroom -

✳ WHEELER DEALERS

On the auction block, this rare, Willy's Coupe from the late 1930s. (Photograph by Henry Lehn)

When driving around Palm Springs you'll see every car that your parents and grandparents ever owned. Even more in the last weekend of February, which is when the annual McCormick's Exotic Car Auction takes place across from the Convention Center. Some 600 beauties are put on display for classic car lovers to get revved up about. Maybe you'll drive home in that red T-Bird with the porthole window? Or that white Chrysler Imperial convertible with maroon leather seats? Then again, a Ford Woody?

detour

HOLE IN THE WALL
North Indian Canyon Drive and Garnet Road

There aren't a lot of bugs in the Coachella Valley due to high winds. But there is this humongous, 28-foot-tall black widow spider made from a vintage Volkswagen Beetle. Its creator was Robert Miner, who from the 1970s to the

1990s owned this auto repair shop called Hole in the Wall. While it's no longer a garage, Miner's daughter and her family now call it home. It's on the left side of North Indian Canyon Drive, just before the Interstate 10 overpass.

- McCormick's Auto Showroom -

Miralon

North Indian Canyon Drive and Miralon Way, North Palm Springs

Miralon is an upscale, 309-acre "agrihood" that opened in 2019. It's on the windy side of town near the wind turbines. The development, which features 1,150 modernist units, has everything you'd expect in a gated desert complex. Except a golf course. And yet there was one. Prior to the 2008 recession, an 18-hole course was built to attract buyers to an upcoming development called Avalon, which didn't happen. When Miralon was built a decade later, the neglected golf course was converted to an olive grove. Who

From golf to olives.

needed another golf course when studies showed that Palm Springs and the Coachella Valley already had more than 120 of them? Watering and upkeep of a golf course is expensive and not drought-friendly. In fact, your typical 18-hole golf course uses 2.08 billion gallons of water a day. More so, studies showed young people aren't that much into the game. It's their parents and grandparents's thing, not theirs — golf couture and costly green fees. So, out went the golf course and in its place a grove of 7,000 olive trees was planted. The fruit is harvested and turned into olive oil by the Temecula Olive Oil Company and sold in markets. Miralon residents receive an allotment of olive oil as part of their homeowner fees.

- Miralon -

Mizell Center
480 South Sunrise Way, Midtown

What once was a fire station at the northeast corner of Ramon Road and South Sunrise Way was redesigned by local **architect Chris Mills**. Its metamorphosis into the sunset-hued Mizell Center was completed in 1991 and named for the late Aaron "Budd" Mizell and his wife, Judge Ruth Bard Mizell. The couple donated $1.4 million to its repurposing. The Mizell Center's 12,000 square feet includes a dining room, auditorium, exercise rooms, meeting rooms, performance spaces and creative arts classes.

I asked Mills what his biggest challenge was in converting this structure to a senior citizen center: "To be a building geared toward seniors, it had to be easy to get around in. That's why there's one main hallway, with everything else feeding off that. There had to be lots of natural light, which meant windows and skylights. We replaced the doors for the fire trucks to go in and out of with a glass wall, which is now in the dining room."

PERSONAL NOTE: It seems that people do not grow older in Palm Springs. Like cactus lilies, they bloom throughout the night. Mary, my neighbor, who's in her late 80s, goes several times a week to take stretch and yoga classes at the Mizell. Afterward, she and her Mizell pals head over to the Tropicale bistro for coconut mojitos. Roberta Linn, who was Lawrence Welk's first Champagne Lady, was still doing local singing gigs in 2023. Just after moving into my condo, my next-door neighbor, Betty, who's in her 90s, introduced herself, telling me that she performs with a band on weekends at the Mizell and that I should come hear her. "You play piano?" I asked. "No," she replied, "drums."

- Mizell Center -

Moorten Botanical Garden

1701 South Palm Canyon Drive, The Mesa

This prickly paradise was founded in 1955 by landscapers Chester "Cactus Slim" Moorten and his wife Patricia. It boasts some 3,000 examples of cacti and other desert plants, and is home to several giant land tortoises.

Located at the entrance to South Palm Canyon Drive, it's the only commercial business in The Mesa neighborhood. Before getting into the landscaping business, Cactus Slim was a celebrated contortionist and Keystone Kop in Mack Sennett's silent film comedies. Patricia was a biologist with a special interest in botany. After relocating to Palm Springs in 1938, they began exploring the surrounding area and collecting desert plants. And not just from the Sonoran Desert but from deserts around the world. Walt Disney bought his plants for Frontier Land from them. Cactus Slim's house was built in 1929 for Stephen H. Willard, who is considered to have been the finest scenic photographer of his era.

Moorten's son, Clark, can be found at the front gate welcoming visitors. For as long as anyone can remember, he has only charged a $5 entry fee per person. "This is not about making money but sharing it with others," he told me. You can even bring your dog along if leashed. As a teenager, Clark helped build the Palm Springs Aerial Tramway and did landscaping jobs for Frank Sinatra and other celebrities. Clark has a sense of humor as dry as the desert.

Clark Moorten

Me: *"Pretty hot today."*
Clark: *"Sure is. It's over 105 out here so I'm closing up."*
Me: *"As they say, at least it's a dry heat."*
Clark: *"Yeah, so's a blowtorch."*

- Moorten Botanical Garden -

Mount San Gorgonio

The mountain peak you see to the north of town is Mount San Gorgonio. At 11,503 feet, it's the highest mountain in Southern California (669 feet higher than Mount San Jacinto). It lies within the San Gorgonio Wilderness and is part of the Sand to Snow National Monument. San Gorgonio ranks seventh highest among peaks in the contiguous 48 U.S. states. Because its peak is significantly above the tree line, it provides for a dramatic snow cap. It was named after Saint Gorgonius of Nicomedia by Spanish missionaries in the 17th century. A martyr, Gorgonius died a terrible death. You don't want to know. The Cahuilla Indians call the mountain Kwiria-Kaich, which means bald or smooth.

Two Rat-Packers united in tragedy

Dolly Sinatra, Frank Sinatra's mother, died on Jan. 6, 1977, when the private Learjet she was on crashed during a snowstorm into Mount San Gorgonio four minutes after leaving Palm Springs Airport. She and a friend were on their way to see her son's opening-night act in Las Vegas. Killed, too, were the jet's two pilots. Frank was informed of his mother's death shortly before his 9 p.m. show. Did he go on? "Of course, he reacted. But he went on anyway," said his manager, Sandy Gallin. "Yeah, and he sounded great. He did the second show, too."

Ironically and tragically, San Gorgonio is the same mountain where 10 years later, March 21, 1987, Dean Martin's second oldest son, Dean Jr., died when the jet plane he was flying crashed into it. He was a member of the California National Air Guard. Dean Jr. was an actor and pop singer and had been married to actress Olivia Hussey (1971-78) and Olympic skater Dorothy Hamill (1982-84). It's said his death destroyed Dean, who after the accident refused to come back to Palm Springs, where he had a house in New Las Palmas.

- Mount San Gorgonio -

Mount San Jacinto

The jagged mountain top you see towering over Palm Springs is Mount San Jacinto, which is 10,834 feet high, just 669 feet less than Mount San Gorgonio, Southern California's tallest peak. Mount San Jacinto is the dividing line between coastal California and the Sonoran Desert. If you'd like to experience the breathtaking view from atop Mount San Jacinto, you can do that via the Palm Springs Aerial Tramway. Feeling athletic, you can hike nine-miles eastward on the Deer Spring Trail that beings in the town of Idyllwild. If you're in Olympic shape, you can hike 11-miles on the vertiginous Cactus to Clouds Trail that begins its ascent at the Palm Springs Art Museum parking lot.

PERSONAL NOTE: A New York friend of mine said that when he first came to Palm Springs, he arrived after dark. The next morning, he told the concierge how surprised he was to look out his window and see all the skyscrapers that were going up here. After a moment the befuddled concierge replied, "Sir, those aren't skyscrapers, those are mountains."

- Mount San Jacinto -

Movie Colony & Movie Colony East

There are two Movie Colonies in Palm Springs, the Movie Colony and the Movie Colony East. The Movie Colony is where, in the mid-1920s and 1930s, Hollywood stars and execs had Spanish Colonial Revivalist estates. The heart of it is between North Indian Canyon Drive and North Via Miraleste, where Ruth Hardy Park is. Movie Colony residents included the likes of Gloria Swanson, Clara Bow, Busby Berkeley, Darryl F. Zanuck, Harold Lloyd, Jack Benny and Cary Grant. An impish friend of mine, Mickey Lang, who grew up in the Movie Colony, told me, "When I was out walking and a tour bus would go by, I'd shield my face with my hands and pick up my pace. Everyone on the bus thought they'd spotted a celebrity, but who?"

Movie Colony East

The Movie Colony East is as different from the older Movie Colony as a fiberglass speedboat is from a Chris-Craft yacht. It was developed, for the most part, after World War II and attracted the younger stars. Located east of Ruth Hardy Park, just across Avenidas Caballeros, it's an eclectic mix of abodes that include some of the most gorgeous mid-century modern houses in Palm Springs. The Movie Colony East was home to stars like Betty Grable, Van Johnson, George Reeves, Bob Hope, Bing Crosby and Frank Sinatra. Lot sizes are modest with few privacy walls. The houses here are one-story to preserve mountain views and to keep neighbors from looking into backyards and swimming pools. Being so close to each other created a party atmosphere. Sinatra would hoist a flag at cocktail hour that meant come on over. It's said that the stars here were a friendly lot that used to come out and greet the tourist buses. It was a different world.

✳ WHY DID THE STARS COME TO PALM SPRINGS?

For starters, blame it on our year-round sunshine. Starting in 1917, Hollywood began shooting films here, especially silent westerns. Perfect weather meant no delays or reshoots. Movie contracts often stipulated that when actors were working in Hollywood, they had to stay within 100 miles of the studio so they could be on call. From Palm Springs, they could be back in a few hours. Stars weren't hassled here. It's rumored that Hollywood photographers stayed away because the studios would blacklist them if they took photos of their clients. Stars didn't have to isolate themselves. They shopped, played golf and dined out. Elvis Presley and Lucille Ball even had their names in the white pages of the phone book. So, too, did Cary Grant, only it was under his birth name, Archibald Leach.

✳ WHERE'D THEY GO?

Today's superstars prefer to live in luxurious golf communities such as The Madision Club in La Quinta, where you'll find members of the Kardashian-Jenner family and Apple CEO Tim Cook. At Bighorn in Palm Desert, you'll run into Mary Hart and producers Jerry Weintraub and Burt Sugarman. Houses in these communities can cost up to $42 million.

- Movie Colony and Movie Colony East -

Museum Trail

Palm Springs Art Museum, 101 N. Museum Drive, Historic Tennis District

Going up? Elven miles to the Ranger Station.

The warning signs you see at the far-right corner of the Palm Springs Art Museum's north parking lot is where the Museum Trail and the Cactus to Clouds Hike begin. Take caution say the signs as you head out: dehydration, heatstroke, sudden and severe weather changes, slippery dirt, dangerous cliffs, oncoming horses and rattlesnakes could await you. The two-mile, round-trip Museum Trail takes you 831 feet up the mountainside, where you'll find picnic tables and sweeping views. Just know that it can be a slippery slope. It's here that the Museum Trail intersects the Skyline Trail, which ascends 7,900 feet to the ranger station at the Palm Springs Aerial Tramway Mountain Station. Called the Cactus to Clouds Hike, it's 11 miles each way and is one of the steepest trails in the nation. Hikers have died on it, and at night you can see helicopters rescuing stragglers. If you do complete the hike and still have energy, you can continue onward from the ranger station to the peak of Mount San Jacinto, which is 10,834 feet high.

- Museum Trail -

Musicland Hotel

1342 South Palm Canyon Drive, Southwest Palm Springs

Originally called the Casa Blanca Hotel, it was remodeled in 1970 and re-christened Musicland. With this project, **architect Hugh Kaptur** created a signature look: long, narrow, recessed windows. You can also see them at Kaptur Plaza. "I differed from my mid-century contemporaries in that I like windows to be attractive architectural features of a building and not just windows with aluminum frames around them. I created niches to hide the air conditioning units," Kaptur told me. He also differed from his contemporaries in that he preferred thick adobe walls to keep out the desert heat, reasoning that the Indians and Spaniards knew best when it came to keeping interiors cool.

- Musicland Hotel -

✳ CHECKING OUT

Musicland was owned in the 1960s by Albert Adamson, a prolific director of such sleaze indies as "Psycho-A-Go-Go," "Blazing Stewardesses," "I Spit on Your Corpse," and "Satan's Sadists." His wife, Regina Carrol, was one of his stars. He met the buxom blond at a restaurant where she was a waiting on tables, and he instantly recognized her B-movie star potential. Adamson's cast members were a ragtag group of over-the-hill actors, motorcyclists and down -and-outs that he housed at the Musicland. Adams retired from filmmaking in the early '80s. After Carrol died of cancer at age 49 in 1992, Adamson recast himself as a house flipper. He was reported missing in 1995. Five weeks later, the 64-year-old's remains were found at the house he was fixing up in Indio buried beneath the cement floor of the bathroom Jacuzzi. Adamson was murdered by his longtime handyman, who was living at the house and on Adamson's credit cards. After Adamson threatened to turn him into the police, the handyman, Fred Fulford, 46, grabbed his hammer and bludgeoned Adamson to death. He was apprehended in Florida, where he had fled. The contractor served 25 years in prison.

- Musicland Hotel -

no

What to SEE in Palm Springs

North Palm Canyon Fuel

2796 North Palm Canyon Drive, North Palm Springs

Also called the Tramway Shell Gas Station, it was awarded historical preservation status in 2016. That's because it's one of the last mid-century gas stations in Palm Springs. It was designed in 1964 by William F. Cody, a refined minimalist. Cody, who was famous for building houses that complemented the desert landscape, put the same thought and detail into this elegant service station. Sadly, it isn't quite the artistic gem it once was. Because of urban growth, it's no longer surrounded by desert sand to make it stand out. Somewhere along the way its landscaped cactus garden was turned into a snack shop. Still, there's the floating roof and large clerestory  windows that define mid-century structures. This Shell station preceded Albert Frey and Robson Chambers's nearby Enco station (2901 North Palm Canyon Drive), which is now the Palm Springs Visitors Center.

Oasis Hotel
125 South Palm Canyon Drive, Downtown

Don't walk past it. Hidden in an alleyway in the heart of downtown is a historically protected art deco tower designed by Lloyd Wright, son of architect Frank Lloyd Wright. The tower is on the west side of South Palm Canyon Drive, just steps from Tahquitz Canyon Way. At three stories and 40 feet high, the tower was for many years the tallest structure in Palm Springs. It was part of the high-end Oasis Hotel, which was commissioned in 1924 by Pearl McCallum McManus and her husband, Austin McManus. The piece of land Pearl chose to place the hotel on is the very site where her father, John McCallum, Palm Springs's first permanent white settler, had the family home built. The hotel's most distinguished feature was the tower, a beacon to her late father. It provided access to upper floors and a rooftop terrace where you were likely to find Loretta Young hanging out, as the Oasis was her favorite place to stay in town. Pearl and Austin, unable to make a financial go of the hotel, sold it in 1927. Pearl retained the right to move her old house should it ever be threatened with demolition. In 1952, she did just that. She had the house taken down brick by brick and reassembled on land she donated to the city at 221 South Palm Canyon Drive, site of the Village Heritage Center. The adobe abode is home to the Palm Springs Historical Society. The modernist Oasis Building, designed by E. Stewart Williams, replaced most of the hotel. It, too, is historically protected. Check out the floating staircase in the back parking lot.

- Oasis Hotel -

Ocotillo Lodge
111 East Palm Canyon Drive, South Palm Springs

The Ocotillo Lodge is a mid-century masterpiece. Completed in 1956, its visionary credentials are impeccable: Designed by architect William Krisel, built by the Alexander Construction Company and landscaped by Garrett Eckbo, who was an advocate for the underdog and middle class.

The Ocotillo Lodge was built for two reasons:

1. To attract potential buyers for the Twin Palms Estates neighborhood, which Krisel and the Alexanders created and which is across the road from the south side of the lodge. The idea was that potential house buyers could stay at the Ocotillo and check out the model homes.

2. To lure the younger Hollywood celebrity clientele to this premier luxury destination. Stars like Elizabeth Taylor, Rock Hudson and Tab Hunter gave it a flashy glamor.

When the Ocotillo opened, it contained 124 rooms and private bungalows that had the conveniences of a home: kitchen, bedroom, living room and walled-in patio. Much of the lodge's allure was its central courtyard, which contains Krisel's key-shaped swimming pool. The Ocotillo also boasted the swank Candlewood Room where A-list entertainers once performed. Located on the second level, the room, which is now a lobby, overlooks the pool and patio area and offers sweeping views of the San Jacinto Mountains. In its heyday, it was billed as America's most beautiful showroom.

The lodge is now condos. It gets its name from the stick-like ocotillo plant, which is also called a candlewood plant.

The lodge first changed ownership in March 1963, when Gene Autry bought it. When it came to business ventures, this singing cowboy didn't horse around. Autry owned the swank Parker Hotel (then California's first Holiday Inn) on

Highway 111 South. He also owned the the Los Angeles Angels baseball team. When Autry decided to relocate the Angels' spring training ground from Phoenix to Palm Springs, he bought the Ocotillo as a place for the players to stay. Autry maintained a suite at the far northeastern corner of the lodge, the only one with a private pool.

Los Angeles Lakers owner Jerry Buss purchased the Ocotillo from Autry in 1968 and owned it through the 1990s. The lodge acquired a rejuvenated buzz with the likes of Magic Johnson and Kareem Abdul-Jabbar staying there. Buss operated his office poolside in his bathing suit. His female assistants also wore bathing suits. New York DJ Jonathan Schwartz likes to tell the story of how his stay there was interrupted one early morning by someone playing electronic rock. He traced the source of the music to a bungalow on the other side of the pool from him. Opening the door, he found Mick Jagger and the Stones jamming "Honky Tonk Women."

In the early 2000s, the bungalows were converted to private ownership and vacation rentals. Bungalow 349 still has Peggy Lee's name on the door. Stars could lease a suite year-round for $3,900.

✳ STICK FIGURES

The ocotillo by any other name (candlewood, coachwhip, slimwood, desert coral, Jacob cactus, vine cactus) is one of Palm Springs's finest looking sculptures. It can be found in many gardens here. An ocotillo is not a true cactus but more related to tea and blueberry plants. It appears to be an arrangement of large spiny dead sticks for most of the year. And what beautiful sticks they are, worthy of a pedestal in any museum of modern art. Their long pointy stems produce beautiful crimson blossoms in the spring and fall, and after a rainfall, small green ovate leaves appear.

- Ocotillo Lodge -

Ojo del Desierto

412 West Tahquitz Canyon Way, Historic Tennis Club District

The Mediterranean Revivalist house that you see above the Palm Springs Art Museum belonged to Texas millionaire Thomas O'Donnell. When completed in 1925 it was named Ojo del Desierto ("Eye of the Desert" in Spanish). Until the 1960s, it was the house with the highest elevation in Palm Springs. The luxurious casa was designed by William Charles Tanner, a painter, muralist, magazine illustrator and architectural designer. He indeed wore many hats. His structures here include the Invernada Estate in the Movie Colony and Nellie Coffman's long-gone, 33 -acre Desert Inn, where Downtown Park is today. Ojo del Desierto was built by master carpenter and developer Alvah Hicks. His resume includes Our Lady of the Solitude Church, Liberace's The Cloisters and Ruth Hardy's Ingleside Inn.

The two-story, 4,200-square-foot house sits on 15 acres of land that was originally leased from Nellie Coffman. Despite the house's generous size, it has a small kitchen and no swimming pool. Didn't matter. The O'Donnells took most of their meals at the Desert Inn, where they also swam in its pool. The promontory rock wall that you see to the north of the house was to be Thomas's burial site. Inside the rock wall is a crypt. California law forbids, however, burial on private land. Thomas, who died in 1945 at age 74, is instead buried at Forest Lawn Cemetery in Glendale. Ojo del Desierto is now known as The O'Donnell House and is owned by the adjacent resort, The Willows Historic Palm Springs Inn. The house, with its terraces, verandas, and gardens, is an historic site and is now used for private parties, corporate retreats, special events and weddings.

- Ojo del Desierto -

One Eleven Vintage Cars
335 East Sunny Dunes Road, Vintage District

If you love classic cars, drive slowly when passing One Eleven Vintage Cars, across from KFC (see: KFC). These blue and orange beauties are 1955 hardtop Chevrolet Bel Aires. Check out the hood emblems that resemble jet airplanes.

FUN FACT

Just how much do we love cars in Palm Springs? To celebrate the city's 85th birthday (it was Saturday, April 8, 2023) a parade of 85 cars, one for every year from 1938 to 2023, made its way through downtown, culminating at the feet of our Forever Marilyn statue. Sticking out among the coupes and convertibles were military Jeeps from the World War II years when cars weren't being produced. Oldest car in the parade — and the hardest to locate — was a 1938 Chevrolet Master Deluxe Convertible that was brought here from Idaho. (Event organized by local car auctioneer Keith McCormick.)

Our Lady of Guadalupe Church
204 South Calle El Segundo, Midtown

Construction of Palm Springs's oldest church, Our Lady of Guadalupe, began in 1911. The Agua Caliente Indians donated the site to the Catholic Church and asked that mass be celebrated there. The church, in California mission style, isn't the original, though. Groundbreaking for this one took place in March, 1963. In front of the church is a statue of Saint Kateri Tekakwitha (1656-1680), who is known as "The Lily of the Mohawks." In 2012 she became the first native American to be canonized as a saint. She is the patroness of ecology and the environment. Every July 4th there's a memorial for her at Our Lady of the Guadalupe Church.

- Our Lady of Guadalupe Church -

Our Lady of Solitude Church
151 West Alejo Road, Uptown

This mission-revivalist Catholic church is one of the oldest places of worship in the Coachella Valley. It had its first service in February 1930. It was designed by architect and engineer Albert Martin, who built such Los Angeles landmarks as City Hall and the Million Dollar Theater. The developer was Alvah Hicks, who built his house, The Cloisters, just up the street on Alejo Road, which is where Liberace died. The church pops up in the closing scene of the 2013 movie "Behind the Candelabra," in which Michael Douglas plays the flamboyant pianist. You can see Matt Damon, who portrays Liberace's estranged lover, Scott Thorson, enter the church to attend the showman's funeral. Because of that scene, people think Liberace's funeral took place there, but it was actually at Forest Lawn Hollywood Hills. A memorial service was held here for Liberace a few days after his passing. There is a plaque inside the church dedicated to him.

FUN FACT

Our Lady of Solitude was popular with many of the Hollywood greats who came to Palm Springs in its formative years. When President Kennedy was in town, he attended services here.

- Our Lady of Solitude Church -

10

What to SEE in Palm Springs

Palm Springs Aerial Tramway

1 Tramway Road, North Palm Springs

You need to take Tram Way Road to get to the Palm Springs Aerial Tramway. It starts at the Visitors Center on Highway 111. It's also known as Lonesome Road since it appears to be going nowhere. Hardly. At the end is the tram, one of the engineering wonders of the world. It was opened in September 1963, 30 years in the making. The project began with Frances Crocker, who was manager of the Palm Springs office of the Electric Power Company. The "father of the tram" never gave up on his dream. He brought together the superstars of Palm Springs modernist architects — Albert Frey, Robson Chambers, John Porter Clark and E. Stewart Williams — to produce the stunning mid-century station buildings.

The original planned map of the Palm Springs Aerial tramway. (Photograph courtesy of the Palm Springs Historical Society - All Rights Reserved)

Upon arriving at the tram's parking lot, you get into an open-air bus that takes you to the Valley Station, which is 2,643 feet above sea level. It's here you board a rotating tram car that transports you to the Mountain Station at 8,516 feet. Capable of holding 80 passengers, these cars are the largest rotating tram cars in the world. The journey takes 12.5 minutes.

- Palm Springs Aerial Tramway -

The Mountain Station is part of Mount San Jacinto State Park. The panoramic view from up there is, of course, breathtaking: windmills, Salton Sea, the Palm Springs grid. From the west end of the building, there is access to hiking and nature trails in the alpine wilderness of Long Valley. In the winter, snowball time. Mountain Station contains a small theater where you can see a documentary on the building of the tramway, which began in August 1962 after decades of dreams and planning. In the year 2000, the rotating cars replaced the original, smaller cars. Also at the summit are two restaurants and, should you need a little something for the trip back down, a full bar.

PERSONAL NOTE: I'm always telling tourists that the tram is a must. Some who won't take it say it's because they have vertigo. When I tell tourists the tram is not scary, that I ride it all the time, I'm telling the truth. The cars do not dangle over Chino Canyon. They hug the side of it, so you always feel there is earth just below your feet. You're never more than 40 to 80 feet from the dirt below. The cars do dip a bit when they hit the support towers so be prepared to go "ewwwww" with everyone else. If you're lucky, you'll be on a car where the operator is playing Neil Diamond's "Sweet Caroline." When the dips come, everyone sings, "So good, so good." And it is.

FUN FACT

The building of the tram could not have been done without helicopters — in this case a fleet of Bell 47G-3Bs sporting 280hp engines. Helicopters were the only way to get cables and other materials to various points along the rugged Chino Canyon cliff sides. It is estimated that more than 23,000 helicopter trips were made with more than 5,500 tons of material being delivered. And not a single crash or serious injury.

SIGHTSEEING TIP: Best to book on-line to avoid long waits (pstramway.com) Even if temperatures on the desert floor are in the triple digits, bring a sweater or jacket. At almost 11,000 feet above sea level, temps can be 40 degrees cooler than on the valley floor.

- Palm Springs Aerial Tramway -

Palm Springs Air Museum
745 North Gene Autry Trail, East Palm Springs

Looking up you may see a F 4U Corsair. (Photograph by Henry Lehn)

The historic fighter planes that you see parked in front of the Palm Springs Air Museum on Gene Autry Trail are just a preview of what's inside the hangars. The nonprofit museum, which opened on Veterans Day 1996, has some 60 warbirds from World War II, the Korean War and the Vietnam War, all restored and in gleaming condition. They include a Boeing B-17 World War II bomber, a British Supermarine Spitfire, a P-51 Mustang and a Grumman FGF Hellcat. Along with the planes, there are displays, exhibits, reading material and docents to tell you all about these aircraft. Some of the docents are military pilots who flew these types of planes. Every Memorial Day, a B-25 Mitchell bomber flies over the museum, then opens its bay door. No need to take cover. The plane drops some 3,000 red and white carnations in remembrance of veterans who gave their lives for their country. Even if you don't go into the museum, you'll hear and see these vintage planes in the skies over Palm Springs. Sometimes they're in squadrons, as if it's December 1941 and our boys are off to fight for freedom.

- Palm Springs Air Museum -

There is a charge to go inside the museum, which is open daily from 10 a.m. to 5 p.m. You can book a flight on various fighters, from an open cockpit bi-winger to a Lockheed T-33 Shooting Star Jet, just like Tom Cruise piloted in "Top Gun." Prices for a ticket to ride vary depending on the aircraft, from $150 to more than $5,000. Above, Museum entrance, below, Mikoyan-Gurevich MiG-17.

- Palm Springs Air Museum -

WINGED VICTORY

SIGHTSEEING TIP: You can see vintage war planes without going into the Air Museum building. Free outdoor displays include a WWII Red Cross ambulance, a bazooka rocket launcher and a military searchlight. Soaring above is a Mustang "Bunny" photographed by Henry Lehn.

- Palm Springs Air Museum -

Palm Springs Animal Shelter

4575 East Mesquite Avenue, East Palm Springs

In Palm Springs, it seems most everything is mid-century modern, including our pets. Built in 2011 and deigned by **architect James Cioffi**, the Palm Springs Animal Shelter is a new take on our modernist tradition. Check out the building's slanted roofs, its metal front sunscreen and the palm trees growing through an opening in the front foyer — just as they do in Albert Frey's City Hall design. The shelter's cement plaster exterior wall sports a vertical raked finish that complements our rocky, sandy terrain. A sleek blue cat and an enormous fuchsia poodle sporting a fancy hairdo greet "forever home" adopters. The metal sculptures are named Mademoiselle Coco and Monsieur Pompadour — the artists are Rancho Mirage residents Karen and Tony Barone. You can see their whimsical, larger-than-life animal works all over the Coachella Valley. To see the shelter, take Ramon Road heading east until you come to South Vella Road, then hang a right. Continue until South Vella ends at East Mesquite Avenue. It's next to Demuth Park.

- Palm Springs Animal Shelter -

Palm Springs Art Museum
101 North Museum Drive, Historic Tennis District

The bold three-story building you see behind Marilyn Monroe is the Palm Springs Art Museum. Located at the base of Mount San Jacinto on Museum Way, its emphasis is on photography and contemporary, regional, Native American and classic American Western art. You can see the museum in one visit and not be overwhelmed. Formerly called the Palm Springs Desert Museum, it's been around and in different locations since 1938. This building was completed in 1962 and was designed by E. Stewart Williams, one of Palm Springs's most celebrated modernists, the designer of Frank Sinatra's Twin Palms house in Movie Colony East. This museum was Williams's favorite contribution to Palm Springs. He wanted the rock façade to complement its mountain backdrop. A perfectionist, he travelled to Oregon where he found just the right volcanic rock. Even though the building is three stories high, it doesn't hinder views. That's because the first floor is sunken. The museum is also home to the 430-seat Annenberg Theater, which presents live performances, lectures and film screenings.

- Palm Springs Art Museum -

Art or bad parking?

detour

CABOT'S PUEBLO MUSEUM
67616 Desert View Avenue, Desert Hot Springs

For a completely different artistic experience, check out Cabot's Pueblo Museum in Desert Hot Springs. It was the residence of Cabot Yerxa, a desert pioneer who died in 1967 and dedicated much of his life to building his abode by hand. Owned now by the City of Desert Hot Springs, it's filled with all kinds of fine and funky treasures, from personal household items to oil paintings he did when he studied art in France. Yerxa discovered hot and cold aquifers beneath his acreage, which led to the development of spas in Desert Hot Springs.

- Palm Springs Art Museum -

Palm Springs City Hall
3200 East Tahquitz Canyon Way, Airport

The main entrance to City Hall resembles an oasis with palm trees growing through a circular hole in the roof.

As you're starting to drive down East Tahquitz Canyon Way from the airport, you're going to see the Palm Springs City Hall on your right. It's an appropriate welcome to this mid-century mecca, as it was designed by the "father of desert modernism," Swiss-born Alfred Frey. Its playful minimalist look was the inspiration for many future Palm Springs commercial buildings and houses. Completed in 1956, City Hall is, as one architectural critic put it, "a structure simple in form, pure in intent and sensitive to its surroundings."

Frey's mentor was the French-Swiss architect and furniture designer, Le Corbusier. Frey, like Le Corbusier, loved experimenting with post-war building materials such as concrete and steel. City Hall's front wall is covered by a screen that has since been duplicated on many mid- century buildings and houses here. It's made of metal tubing cut at angles and stacked in rows. More than visually

As you enter City Hall you're greeted by the "Palm Springs Rose," which was introduced by Constance Elmer and donated to the city in 1945.

- Palm Springs City Hall -

arresting, it shields the building against the intense morning sun. Large canopies over City Hall's entrances provide shade. As if entering an oasis, its main entrance has tall palm trees growing through its center canopy.

Assisting Frey on its design and construction were upcoming mid-century architects E. Stewart Williams, Robson C. Chambers and John Porter Clark.

The alternate entrance to City Hall is a portico with the motto: The People Are the City.

SIGHSEEING TIP: If you're near City Hall, walk or drive over to the police headquarters, which is off East Tahquitz Canyon Way at 200 South Civic Drive. The Palm Springs Police Officers Association Memorial Plaza is in front of the building. In the middle of it you'll find a life-size bronze sculpture of two police officers entitled "Help Is on the Way" — one of the officers is down and the other is summoning assistance. The work is by local sculptor Jeffrey Fowler and is dedicated to "those in law enforcement."

FUN FACT

Le Corbusier (1887-1965) is considered by many to be the world's most important modernist architect. It's said that all roads of modernism lead to him. Of Swiss and French citizenship, his projects included the United Nations headquarters in New York and the Chapel of Notre-Dame-du-Haut in Ronchamp, France, which the Bank of America on South Palm Canyon Drive is modeled after. Although Le Corbusier never came to Palm Springs, he was the mentor to our desert modernists architects. He inspired them by telling them that the desert was their canvas to create upon.

- Palm Springs City Hall -

Palm Springs Community Church

283 South Cahuilla Road, Historic Tennis District

Two suspicious fires (Sept. 18, 2013, and April 22, 2022) destroyed much of the Palm Springs Community Church that's locate in the Historic Tennis District. (Palm Springs has a history of suspicious fires.) Built in 1935, the Gothic structure was designed by renaissance man William Charles Tanner, a painter, muralist, magazine illustrator, and architectural designer. His structures here include Ojo del Desierto above the Palm Springs Art Museum, the Invernada mansion in the Movie Colony, and Nellie Coffman's long-gone, 33-acre Desert Inn. On February 21, 1954, President and Mrs. Eisenhower worshiped in the church during a week-long visit to Palm Springs. The church was designated a Class 1 historic site in 1989.

- Palm Springs Community Church -

Palm Springs Convention Center
277 North Avenida Caballeros, Central Palm Springs, Midtown

The west side of the downtown Convention Center looks oddly distorted, as if it were a reflection in a funhouse mirror. Notice its curved, undulating roof line and stone pillars that lean in drunken directions. Yet it wasn't always so unconventional looking. Built in the late 1980s, the Convention Center was originally designed by HNTB of Los Angeles, which specializes in sporting arenas, and constructed by McDivitt & Street of Dallas. In 2005 a metamorphosis occurred. Fentress Architects of Denver, a firm that specializes in big spaces, like airport terminals, completely remodeled and expanded the Convention Center to 261,000-square-feet. Price tag: $34 million. "They really took a nondescript building and converted it to a very Palm Springs structure," says **architect Chris Mills**. When the final re-construction curtain was pulled back, a switcheroo had occurred: The back of the building was now the front of the building, thus providing conventioneers and visitors with breathtaking views of the San Jacinto Mountains and our fiery, Wagnerian sunsets. Says Mills: "If you look at the east side, toward the south side, you see some barrel tile pyramid roofs. That area is all that's left of the previous building." The opening of the Palm Springs International Film Festival, founded by Mayor Sonny Bono in 1990, takes place here every January. Klieg lights illuminate the sky as an international list of stars arrive.

FACT CHECKING: There's a myth that futurist architect William Pereira, who designed San Francisco's Transamerica Pyramid, designed or remodeled our Convention Center. He did neither.

Palm Springs International Airport
3400 East Tahquitz Canyon Way

Tourists come to Palm Springs to relax and unwind. The minute you deplane at the Palm Springs International Airport, that process begins. At the center of the main terminal is an open-air courtyard where the desert's calming air welcomes you like a stiff drink. You've arrived.

The 40,000-square foot main terminal was designed by modernist architect Donald Wexler and completed in 1966. Because of his visionary thinking, the terminal is listed on the National Register of Historic Places. In various travel polls, it's been voted the best small airport in America.

- Palm Springs International Airport -

"Passengers have been forgotten in the air age. We have sought to design this building for the passengers, not the planes," Wexler said decades ago. The passenger terminal consists of three parts: the main building and two concourses, the Sonny Bono concourse being the latest addition in 1999. All walkways connecting these structures are roofless so you can see where you're going without directional signs.

Know this, though: The main terminal isn't quite the architectural jewel it once was. Over the decades it has been altered and neglected. According to Wexler's son, **designer Gary Wexler**, "there is little left of the original design." A Palm Springs preservationist, Gary says that there are plans underway to restore the terminal and that there's been no opposition. Don't hold your breath, though. He says it will take years and years to complete.

The former site of an Army base, the terminal is on land purchased from the Agua Caliente Indians in 1958. The airport covers 940 acres and has two runways. It isn't just for passenger planes. There's a separate terminal for private and corporate jets. Because the airport takes federal dollars, it must allow federal military planes to use the runways. The sound of fighter jets scraping the sky as they head off into the wild blue yonder can be both thrilling and deafening. I know, I live near the airport.

- Palm Springs International Airport -

The airport has a strong military background, having been built as an Army airfield at the start of World War II. Called the Palm Springs Air Base, it was a city within a city, sporting a post office, movie theater, fire station, recreation room, gym and library. It was used as a receiving area for wounded soldiers bound for Torney General Hospital, formerly the El Mirador Hotel. Pilots were trained at the airfield to ferry B-25 bombers, C-47 transport planes and other fighters to military bases and battlegrounds around the world. Because men were needed in combat, many women were trained as pilots to take on these duties.

✳ ARC DE TRIOMPHE

The first thing you see out of your airplane window as you're landing at the Palm Springs airport from the south is the Tahquitz Creek Golf Resort, which was built in 1957. Modernist **architect Hugh Kaptur** designed the clubhouse, whose roof mimics the arc of a golf swing, though he claims not intentionally. "I wanted desert visitors to see something clean and efficient from the air," Kaptur told me, "and the golf course is the first thing you see before landing." A green roof with the golf course's name on it was later added to the center of the structure, which Kaptur says ruins its design. "Can you photoshop it out for me?" he asked. Done.

- Palm Springs International Airport -

Palm Springs Public Library
300 South Sunrise Way, Central Palm Springs

One of the last buildings that architect William F. Cody designed was the Palm Springs Public Library, which opened in 1975. Shortly before that, he designed nearby Saint Theresa of the Child Jesus Church, his masterwork. The library and Saint Theresa's share Cody's love of Japanese minimalism. By their natures, libraries and churches are quiet places. And so, like Saint Theresa, the library's façade is surrounded by a curved granite wall that helps block traffic noise and provides shade. Cody suffered a debilitating stroke in 1973 that ended his career. He died five years later at age 62.

- Palm Springs Public Library -

Palm Springs Sign
North Palm Springs

Visitors driving into Palm Springs on Highway 111 heading south are greeted by the Palm Springs sign, which is just before the Visitors Center. It's a popular spot to stand in front of and get your photo taken. Behind the sign is Chino Canyon and the San Jacinto Mountains.

Look for signs with retro typography on restored hotels and motels.

Many streets and highways here are named after the old stars.

When the desert winds kick up, you can't always get to Desert Hot Springs on Gene Autry Trail or North Indian Canyon Drive.

Palm Springs Tennis Club
701 West Baristo Road, Historic Tennis Club

The Palm Springs Tennis Club is in the heart of the Historic Tennis Club neighborhood. What you're looking at today may look like a medical building in any city. Yet the X-rays show a different story. If it weren't for the influential, trend-setting Pearl McCallum Mc-Manus, daughter of John McCallum, the first full-time white settler in Palm Springs, this area of town would have been called something else. Pearl built one of the first tennis courts in this

area on land she owned and grew up on. Her mountainside pink mansion, overlooking downtown Palm Springs, was here. She died in 1966. In the early 1970s, the mansion was demolished and replaced by the Palm Springs Tennis Club hotel.

"Auntie Pearl," as she was called, and husband Austin McManus realized that Palm Springs and tennis went well together. In 1937, they opened the Palm Springs Tennis Club on their property. It originally had two tennis courts, clubhouse bar, café and swimming pool — not just any swimming pool but one Pearl insisted be oval instead of rectangular. Suddenly, everyone wanted an oval pool. Pearl surrounded the pool and its patio area with palm trees, put in a waterfall and planted gardens lush with bougainvillea. The pool area is still there, an oasis worthy of the chic-est of sheiks.

Over the years, Pearl added more courts and built bungalows to house more guests. After World War II, she hired Paul R. Williams, the first black member of the American Institute of Architects, and architect A. Quincy Jones to in corporate California Modernism into the club's design. Pearl sold the club in 1961. To this day, it has maintained its reputation for having some of the best courts in the world and for attracting the crème de la crème of tennis players. It's also home to Spencer's Restaurant, whose owner, Harold Matzner, named the high-end eatery after his 100-pound Siberian husky.

SIGHTSEEING TIP: If you'd like to see the swimming pool, park on Baristo Road and wander towards Spencer's. The entrance to the pool area is just past the valet parking attendants' station. There are signs around the pool that say no bikinis, thongs or snapping of towels.

✳ HISTORIC NEIGHBORHOOD

The Historic Tennis Club neighborhood sports more preservation plaques than any other area of Palm Springs. Whether driving, biking or hoofing it, this area proves a mellow experience. Most of the Historic Tennis Club area extends from West Ramon Road to the Palm Springs Art Museum. It is bordered by Belardo Road on the east and the San Jacinto Mountains on the west. Here the mountains offer protection from the desert winds and late afternoon sun. It's little wonder why the early white settlers yelled, "Dibs!" upon seeing this area (not that the Cahuilla Indians hadn't been living here for thousands of years). The oldest residences in Palm Springs can be found in this district, many having been converted into boutique hotels that are close to downtown. Scattered amongst the old adobe structures are some suave mid-century condo complexes, too.

A blade sign atop a stop sign at the corner of Arenas and Cahuilla roads.

At the end of West Tahquitz Way is the exclusive Colony 29 (147 South Tahquitz Drive). Built in 1929, the gated complex consists of only seven Spanish -style houses. The Historic Tennis Club neighborhood is where Nellie Coffman's 35-acre resort, the Desert Inn, was. It is now Downtown Park behind the Kimpton Rowan Palm Springs Hotel. This is bike- and foot-friendly territory.

- Palm Springs Tennis Club -

Palm Springs Unified School District
333 South Farrell Drive, Midtown

As sleek and cool as a Hitchcock blond, this school administration building was designed by mid-century minimalist E. Stewart Williams in 1962. His more known works include Frank Sinatra's Twin Palms house in the Movie Colony East, Temple Isaiah, the Palm Springs Art Museum and the Coachella Valley Savings & Loan, which is now a Chase bank. The Chase bank and this building share one of Williams' signature design elements: inverted steel columns.

TACKLING THE HEAT

If you're on Amado Road heading east past the Palm Springs Public Library, you might catch the Palm Springs High School Indians football team in a game or in practice. They hit the field even in the hot summer months. The high school is located at 2401 East Baristo Road.

- Palm Springs Unified School District -

Palm Springs Visitors Center

2901 North Palm Canyon Drive, North Palm Springs

The first building you see coming into Palm Springs on Highway 111 heading south is the Palm Springs Visitors Center, which was an Esso service station when it was completed in 1965. The building's triangular roof, which spans 95 feet, resembles a Stealth bomber and was designed by architects Alfred Frey, the "father of desert modernism," and Robson Chambers. According to a bronze plaque at the Visitors Center, "the roof is a hyperbolic parabo-loid of steel I-beams and corrugated metal roofing supported by steel tubular pillars." The building was also called the Tramway Gas Station because it's at the base of Tramway Road. The Palm Springs Bureau of Tourism has run the building since 2003. Inside is a gift shop, vintage photographs of Palm Springs and the Agua Caliente Indians, and an info booth. It's listed on the USA's National Register of Historic Places (see: North Palm Canyon Fuel).

- Palm Springs Visitors Center -

FUN FACTS

At the first traffic light coming into town on Highway 111 heading south is the Number 1. To help visitors from getting lost, all traffic lights along Route 111, from Palm Springs to Indio, are numbered.

June McCarroll, a nurse and physician whose office was on Highway 111 (then U.S. Route 99) in Indio, watched many head-on collisions from her window. And so, a light bulb went off over her head: Delineate a divided highway by painting a stripe down the middle. Thanks to her undivided attention, divider lines became a global phenomenon starting in 1930. She is memorialized by a stretch of Interstate 10 through Indio named in her honor.

detour

WHITEWATER PRESERVE
9160 Whitewater Canyon Road

Should you need some relief from our desert temps, you can head to higher ground, such as Joshua Tree, Big Bear or Idyllwild. But those are day trips. When I crave cooler air, I drive 14 miles north of the **Visitor's Center** on Highway 111 to Whitewater Preserve. I lived in Palm Springs for years before someone told me about this hidden paradise. It's free, too.

The Whitewater Preserve's 2,851 acres are the backdrop to the 154,000-acre Sand to Snow National Monument that stretches from Mount San Gorgonio to Joshua Tree National Park. After driving on a bumpy, serpentine road you arrive at the entrance to the preserve, where there's a ranger station, grassy lawn, picnic tables, barbecue grills, a camping area and restrooms. Just west of the parking lot is the Whitewater River. When running, its journey from the San Bernardino Mountains to the Coachella Valley is dramatically shepherded by spectacularly steep cliffs that have gravity-defying boulders. Next to the ranger station are serene pools of water that are connected to each other by small waterfalls. These pools used to be stocked with fish. The preserve was until 2016 a trout hatchery. If you arrive on a hot summer day, it's like stepping into a medieval cathedral where the air is cool and the vibe sacred.

- Palm Springs Visitors Center -

The preserve is open all year and, unlike so many parks, dogs are allowed, leashed. There are no trash cans. What you bring in you take back, except for dog waste, for which there is a bin. The preserve has spectacular hiking trails that range from 3.5 to eight miles. You can even switch onto the Pacific Crest National Scenic Trail for a short spell, or continue along it if you'd like to visit Seattle. No pressure to exert yourself at Whitewater, though. You can meander around the old trout ponds, now home to contented coots. You can indulge your feet in a wading pool, see exhibits in the ranger station, or read a book under a ramada of shade trees.

The preserve is home to bighorn sheep, bears, mountain lions and the endangered California red-legged frog and fringe-toed lizard; several bird species, including the willow flycatcher and Least Bell's vireo. Signs along trails warn of rattlesnakes.

To get to the preserve, take Highway 111 North to the Whitewater turnoff. Keep a sharp eye out for the sign, which is on the right side of the highway. Miss it and you'll end up on Interstate 10. Once off 111, you're on Whitewater Canyon Road. Follow to the end, some five miles.

- Palm Springs Visitors Center -

Palm Trees

Palm trees are iconic to Palm Springs, but are they native? They are, but not the tall, swaying kind that line Palm Canyon Drive and that you see throughout the Coachella Valley. Those are Mexican fan palms, native to Northern Mexico. They can grow to 100 feet and live 100 years. They do not produce dates.

The *Washingtonia filifera*, or desert fan palm, is native to this area and can be found around oases, stream beds and at the Agua Caliente Cultural Center. You can see several clusters of them in Andreas and Palm canyons. The Washingtonia was named by a German horticulturist in 1897 in honor of George Washington, whose name is associated with cherry trees. Go figure. At 60 feet tall, washingtonias are shorter than the Mexican fan and have a larger trunk. They don't produce dates, either.

Can you see the worker who climbed this tree?

So, who around here gets dates? That distinction goes to the Phoenix dactylifera, aka the date palm, which is tall and slender and closely resembles the Mexican fan palm. There used to be date farms in Palm Springs, but no more. Most are now outside Indio heading south. The Coachella Valley is the Date Capital of the World, supplying more than 90 percent of dates grown in the United States; that's more than 49,300 tons a year. Why are dates expensive? Date trees need to be pollinated to bear fruit. Because of strong desert winds, there aren't enough bugs to do the job. The date trees must be polli-

nated by hand. Each February, a worker climbs up a male palm tree, cuts off the sheath, dries it until the pollen inside becomes a fine powder and then climbs up the female trees and deposits the powder. A couple of months later, you have dates.

Beginning every summer, our Mexican fan palms get trimmed. Using a pulley system, trimmers laden with heavy buzzsaws and machetes work their way up the trees to cut back dead branches. Trucks with lift buckets are sometimes used if the tree is near a street. Tree trimmers often work in in triple digit temperatures.

FUN FACT

The Coachella Valley has another species of tall, slender palm trees that can reach its maximum height in just a few days. A fine cluster of them can be seen at Vista Chino and North Cerritos Road, near the end of the Palm Springs International Airport's northern runway. Although they are not living palm trees, but cell towers made to look like them, they can produce dates of a different kind.

Park Imperial South

South Palm Springs

A striking example of mid-century, folded-plate roof design can be seen on the left-hand side of Araby Drive, shortly after turning onto it from East Palm Canyon Drive (Highway 111). Called Park Imperial South, this complex was completed in 1960. The three-and-a-half-acre complex has been designated a Historic District. The roofs are made of "stressed skin" prefabricated plywood panels, which allow fewer support walls and columns. It was built by mid-century developers Jack Meiselman and Richard Lewis. The architect, Barry A. Berkus, was only 25 when he designed it. The folded-plate roofs purposely complement the mountains.

- Park Imperial South -

Parkview Mobile Estates
West Mesquite Avenue & Belardo Road, West Palm Springs

An adobe-style mobile home sits next to a mobile farmhouse with a windmill.

Mobile home parks are everywhere in the Coachella Valley. Leave it to Palm Springs to have some of the coolest. We think of mobile home parks as being the antithesis of individuality: long narrow boxes with carports, tiny front yards (often Astroturf) and flower boxes under the front windows. The words "trailer park," according to Wikipedia, "are stereotypically viewed as lower income housing for occupants living in or below the poverty line who have low social status." Not in Palm Springs where style rules.

Parkview Mobile Estates is a great example. Modest of size, the park boasts a gallery of eclectic exteriors that include adobe casas, Alexander moderns, New Orleans colonials and Japanese tea houses. Abutting the base of the San Jacinto Mountains near the entrance to Tahquitz Canyon Falls, Parkview seems isolated but is walking distance to downtown. The neighbors are friendly here, always up for a drink, especially during our summer drought months. The neighbors I'm referring to are bighorn sheep, bobcats, mountain lions, coyotes and what's that rattling sound?

Mobile home parks practically started in Palm Springs. Like caftans, classic T-Birds and pink flamingos, they have a beloved retro vibe. It's gratifying to see so many of the classic trailers from the 1950 and '60s. Some parks have clubhouses for community potluck dinners, special events and movie nights. Other parks are going with the times by selling

- Parkview Mobile Estates -

tiny houses and manufactured homes. Some parks down valley have 18-hole golf courses, public restaurants and nightclubs. Most parks in Palm Springs and the Coachella Valley are listed as "55 and older."

Mobile home parks in Palm Springs began as an affordable, low-maintenance alternative to owning a seasonal house. Now, of course, owners and renters live in them year round. Many sell for hundreds of thousands of dollars and more. Movie stars invested in Coachella Valley trailer parks in the early days. Bing Crosby owned the Blue Skies Village Park in Rancho Mirage, which is still there, and which he named after his hit song "Blue Skies." Although we think of trailer parks as being a 1950s invention, Ramon Park (now called Ramon Mobile Home & RV Park) at Ramon Road and Sunrise Way, has been a part of Palm Springs since 1937. It vies for being the country's first trailer park. Vocalist and "Touched by an Angel" star Della Reese lived there.

✳ MOVIE TRAILER

Lucille Ball and Desi Arnaz are largely responsible for mobile homes becoming an American mainstay. After their movie "The Long, Long Trailer" came out in 1954, trailer sales across America went through the roof. Some of that movie was filmed on vertiginous Highway 74, the twisty "Pines to Palms" scenic route that begins in Palm Desert. For the record, Lucy and Ricky's trailer was a 1953 36-foot Redman New Moon, which sold for $5,345. The car that towed their trailer was a 1953 Mercury Monterey convertible with a 125 horsepower flathead V8 engine. You need that power going up Highway 74.

- Parkview Mobile Estates -

Pearl McCallum Fountain
Palm Springs Airport

Pearl McCullum McManus (Photograph courtesy of the Palm Springs Historical Society - All Rights Reserved)

The stone fountain in front of the Palm Springs International Airport honors Pearl McCallum McManus, the first non-Indian child in Palm Springs. She was the daughter of John Guthrie McCallum, the first permanent white settler. Referred to as "Auntie Pearl," she was one of the city's most influential residents and developers. She died in 1966 at age 87. The fountain, designed by architect Julio de la Pena of Guadalajara, Mexico, was installed a year later. Its 398 pieces were hand cut from cantera stone in the state of Jalisco. The fountain is not in the mid-century modernist style of the Donald Wexler-designed airport. Purposely so. "The fountain is Mexican in flavor," its creator said upon completion. "It is supposed to be so that people will see it as a symbol of friendship from Mexico."

- Pearl McCullum McManus -

Peter Lawford's House

1295 North Via Monte Vista, Las Palmas

There used to be a plaque in the front of Peter Lawford's house in Vista Las Palmas saying that this is where President John F. Kennedy met Marilyn Monroe. That could be as Lawford, the English-born Rat Pack member was married four times; his first wife was Patricia Kennedy, who was JFK's sister. It's more likely, however, that Monroe met Kennedy at Lawford's house in Santa Monica. As for an affair between Monroe and JFK, many Marilyn historians believe it was merely a one-night stand on March 24, 1962, at Bing Crosby's Rancho Mirage compound. Old-timers here say it wasn't MM that JFK had the hots for but Angie Dickinson, who had a house just up the hill from Lawford's. Dickinson has denied rumors that she had an affair with JFK.

President John Kennedy chatting it up with his sister, Patricia, who was married to Peter Lawford (right).

- Peter Lawford's House -

Piazza di Liberace
1441 North Kaweah Road, Old Las Palmas

You don't need a tour guide to tell you who owned this villa. When you see the mailbox shaped like a black grand piano, the musical notes on the fence and the Roman and Greek statuary, it could only be Liberace. Piazza di Liberace is one of the several residences he owned in Palm Springs. Built in 1952, the three-bedroom, six-bathroom house was bought in 2012 by a medical doctor and her accountant husband who loved the showman. No way were they going to put a privacy hedge around this lollapalooza of a palazzo. They even illuminate the house at night. The tall iron gateway on the front step opens onto a black and white foyer that has a large portrait of the flamboyant pianist posing with an elegant Afghan hound. The painting is framed by two over-sized gold-leafed candelabras. Turning the corner from Kaweah Road onto Camino Norte West you'll see the side of the house is graced by the Statue of

Liberty. The owners told the Desert Sun newspaper that they had fun restoring the 3,100-square-foot house to its original opulence, including ceilings with painted cherubs. The couple said that when they first tried polishing the copper, swan-necked bathroom faucets, they wouldn't polish. Turns out they were solid 14-karat gold.

- Piazza di Liberace -

Popsicles
Historic Tennis District

These colorful, giant popsicles were introduced to Palm Springs in 2017 as part of Desert X, an outdoor contemporary art exhibition that is held every two years in the Coachella Valley. The pop art installation was originally located on a sandy lot on Sunny Dunes Road in the vintage antique district. In 2023 the Palm Springs City Council voted to move the work to a permanent location in Downtown Park.

- Popsicles -

Pumping Stations

Throughout Palm Springs neighborhoods you'll see dirt lots with weird-shaped pipes and other metal forms. Although they look like playgrounds designed by Edward Gorey, they are pumping stations that provide our water. When giving tours people are often confused as to why we have so much greenery here, from gardens and lawns to golf courses. This is, after all, a desert that gets only five-and-a-half inches of rain a year if that. There is, however, a lot of groundwater beneath us. The entire Coachella Valley, from Mt. San Gorgonio in the north to Indio in the south, sits on a giant aquifer that's located 1,200 feet underground, and is managed by the Desert Water Agency. These pumping stations tap into this underground reservoir, transporting water to various locations, including hillside holding tanks. Believe it or not, the Coachella Valley, as recently as 1400 AD, was a fresh-water lake. Seepage from that lake helped create the reservoir. It remains plentiful thanks to the Colorado River, though that supply has become limited due to drought conditions. Water from the river is piped here from Lake Havasu on the Arizona border.

Purple Room Supper Club
1900 East Palm Canyon Drive, South Palm Springs

As you're driving by the marquee for the Purple Room on Highway 111 East (across from the Smoke Tree Commons shopping center), blow it a kiss. The Purple Room supper club is a classy throwback to Palm Springs at its retro best; i.e, booze, nightclubs and the Rat Pack. Located in the tiki-themed Trinidad Hotel, the Purple Room was where the hippest of entertainers performed. The most famous of them was a trio of pals who were never officially booked but on occasion leapt to the stage when the spirits moved them: Frank Sinatra, Dean Martin and Sammy Davis Jr. --- AKA the Rat Pack. The Purple Room was one of Sinatra's favorite "saloons," as he called it. Even when he moved down valley, he would stop at the Purple Room for a drink on his way into town and for a nightcap on his way home. Sometimes he'd call up the club and book the entire room for himself and a party of guests.

The Purple Room is where Frank proposed marriage to his fourth and last wife, Barbara. Tony Curreri, who tended bar in the 1970s, got to be chums with Frank and his extended family. He remembered one evening seeing

Frank's feisty mother, Dolly, sitting alone enjoying a bowl of soup. Her son's tunes were being piped in over the loudspeakers. Dolly motioned Curreri to her table, "Hey, Tony, can you get this guy off" she asked, pointing to the loudspeakers, "he's driving me f-----g crazy!"

Purple Room owner, restaurateur, singer and Judy Garland impersonator, Michael Holmes, has preserved the supper club — one of the last left in America —in all of its retro, highball glory. Almost every night, top singers and jazz musicians perform. During performances, you can have dinner at a table or sit at the bar. You can even book the Dean Martin Booth.

Dean Martin (left), Frank Sinatra (center) and Sammy Davis Jr. (right).

FUN FACT

The Rat Pack reportedly got its start at Humphrey Bogart's house in Los Angeles where actors and singers would meet to hang out. It's said that actress Lauren Bacall thought the guys looked like rats and gave them the name "The Rat Pack."

- Purple Room Supper Club -

What to SEE in Palm Springs

Racquet Club

North Indian Canyon Drive, North Palm Springs

You wouldn't know driving past the vanquished remains of the Racquet Club that it was for decades the star-studded place to stay and play in Palm Springs. Opening in 1934, it was the vision of actors Charles Farrell and Ralph Bellamy. While riding horses at the north end of town, they saw a "For Sale" sign by builder Alvah Hicks on 53 acres of undeveloped land for $3,500. Let's buy it, they agreed, and open our own tennis club. Farrell and Bellamy were known to hog the tennis courts at the El Mirador Hotel, which were reserved for guests.

All that's left of the Racquet Club is the remains of the Bamboo Room.

Besides tennis courts, the Racquet Club had one of the most popular swimming pools in Palm Springs. Olympic size, too. A hot attraction was the legendary bar called the "Bamboo Room" frequented by stars such as Clark Gable, Spencer Tracy, Dinah Shore and Lucille Ball. There was also a dining room with a dance floor, where in the early years Rudy Vallee's orchestra played on Saturday nights. Dues at the Racquet Club weren't cheap by Depression-era standards: $650 apiece for an annual membership. At first, few members joined due to the cost, which Farrell and Bellamy wouldn't lower. That was smart marketing. People began to think If this club is so expensive it must be the place to be. In a few years, everyone wanted to join.

Farrell, who bought out Bellamy early on, encouraged up-and-coming actors to stay at the club to give it a youthful vibe. In 1949, Hollywood pin-up photographer Bruno Bernard brought a 22-year-old Marilyn Monroe here to photograph her by the pool. She got more than photos. William Morris talent agent Johnny Hyde was staying at the Racquet Club at the time. When he saw her being photographed, he was gobsmacked and signed her to her first studio contract. Hyde fell so deeply in love with Monroe that he left his wife and

Marilyn Monroe with pin-up photographer Hugo Bernard at the Racquet Club. This is the first publication of that image (See: Forever Marilyn). (Photograph courtesy of the Palm Springs Historical Society - All Rights Reserved)

four sons for her, even though she continually turned down his marriage proposals. A year after meeting Marilyn, he dropped dead of a heart attack — or was it a broken heart?

The Racquet Club was active until the 1980s. In 2014, a fire destroyed what was left of the once glamorous resort. The Bamboo Room survived with little damage. Because the club was built on private land, it was given historic preservation status and can't be demolished.

PULP FICTION?

Local legend has it that the Bloody Mary cocktail was first concocted in the Bamboo Room. It's apparently not the room where it happened. That honor goes to the New York Bar (now Harry's New York Bar) in Paris. Its inventor was the room's legendary French bartender, Fernand Petiot, who had been making versions of the popular drink there beginning in 1921. In an interview in The New Yorker magazine, Petiot said that he got the idea of mixing tomato juice and vodka during World War I. According to Petiot, American soldiers in France were being sent cans of tomato juice from home. Russians fleeing Russia were bringing vodka with them. He simply combined the two, he said.

- Racquet Club -

Ramon Law Building

1255 East Ramon Road, Midtown

Situated on a modest-sized lot with limited parking and hidden behind trees, flowers and shrubbery is the angular, futuristic Ramon Law Building. Coming upon it is like discovering a parked UFO. I only found out about it when I got a text from my barber to let me know he had moved to Salon Suites, which is in the 2,600 square-foot building. Upon finding it, I was lost in space. Why hadn't this modernist masterpiece been celebrated? I asked its **architect, Chris Mills**, how it came about. "My clients were lawyers," he said. "Their instructions in 1978 were to build a timeless building, one that would appear to be new architecture at any point in time. I used angles to make it modernist from a Palm Springs standpoint."

Revivals
611 South Palm Canyon Drive, Financial District

Revivals is Palm Springs's premier non-profit secondhand store (though they do sell new Mode Furniture). Here's where locals go to get deals on secondhand couches, beds, clothes, art, appliances and housewares. You can often snag barely used, high-end furniture here. As sharp looking as modernist couches and chairs may be, they often aren't very comfy, especially for TV binging. So, after a year or so, they're brought here for adoption. This is the original Revivals. Others have opened in Cathedral City, Palm Desert and Indio. All profits from the four Revivals go to Desert AIDS Project.

- Revivals -

DESERT AIDS PROJECT
1695 North Sunrise Way, Midtown

The buff building that anchors the corner of Vista Chino and Sunrise Way is the Desert AIDS Project, founded in 1984 by community volunteers. It's Coachella Valley's primary not-for-profit resource for those living with, affected by, or at risk for AIDS. DAP moved to this 44,000 square-foot campus in 1998. Its staff consists of 400 volunteers: doctors, specialists, nurses, pharmacists and more. Facilities include a dental clinic, walk-in testing lab and a pharmacy. DAP has grown to offer services that treat mental illness and substance abuse, and it helps provide food and housing to the disadvantaged. During the COVID-19 pandemic, DAP gave free testing to the community. Flying colorfully out front are flags that celebrate Pride and AIDS research.

- Revivals -

Richard Milanovich Memorial Bridge
West Palm Springs

Richard Milanovich (Photo courtesy of Palm
Springs Historical Society. All Rights Reserved)

The bridge on South Belardo Road that crosses the Tahquitz Creek wash is dedicated to the late beloved tribal leader and activist Richard Milanovich. He was chairman of the Agua Caliente Band of Cahuiilla Indians for three decades. Under his leadership, the tribe went from poverty to post-casino wealth. He died in 2012 at age 69. His son, Reid, is now chairman.

HOW WEALTHY ARE TRIBE MEMBERS?

Since the tribe keeps mostly to itself, no one really knows. Since they are their own nation, they pay no federal, state or city taxes, and are exempt from capital gains. In July, 2023, Palm Springs real estate broker Ben Blank told the Desert Sun newspaper, "The Indians, with their wealth, keep a low profile, take pains not to abuse the freedoms they have and are highly respected for their business acumen."

- Richard Milanovich Memorial Bridge -

Robolights

East Granvia Valmonte & Arguilla Road, Movie Colony East

"Oh, do not ask, What is it?
Let us go and make our visit." —T.S. Eliot

When I give a tour and get to this intersection, the response is always the same: disbelief. You're looking at Robolights, Kenny Irwin's surreal art installation that covers every inch of his two-acre urban property. Since living in the desert, I've learned that survival can take uncanny forms, from flowers that bloom only for the moon's delight, to jumping cacti to lizards that swim through the sand to escape predators. And then there's Kenny, a sculptor like no other.

Since Kenny was a child, he's has been converting his family's grounds into a mad, comical, twisted, loving world. His initial theme was "Christmas meets science fiction," which is why you see lots of Santas, reindeer, icicles and giant transformers. His materials are found, discarded and donated objects, including dolls, ceiling fans and shopping carts. People like to feed Kenny's creative appetite by tossing household items over his walls. From your window you can see the tip of the iceberg: A great white shark with a silver candy cane in its jaws, a pastel-colored Ferris wheel, a military tank, the Grinch's Whoville house and enormous robotic figures. Check out the orange light utility vehicle. Kenny inherited it from a neighbor who crashed it into live power lines. He figured Kenny could do something with it. In appreciation, "I pointed it at his house so he could see it," he told me.

The youngest of nine children, Kenny was always encouraged by his late parents to freely express himself. Robolights began when, at age 13, Kenny told his father that he wished more neighbors would put up outdoor holiday lights. His dad encouraged him to do it. Now middle-aged, Kenny has been doing it ever since, only year-round. "I wanted to create a fusion between art and amusement parks," said Kenny, who believes in spreading joy to the world.

Not all of his neighbors are joyful about Robolights. Up until Christmastime 2018, he would open the grounds to the public at night. Thousands of curiosity seekers would come, creating traffic jams, parking problems and litter. In 2019, the Palm Springs Fire Department deemed the 80,000 colored lights that illuminate the installations to be a fire hazard and closed Robolights. Not entirely though. You can arrange a private daytime viewing by googling "Robolights."

Kenny's real dream is to open a horror amusement park on 10 acres he purchased in Desert Hot Springs. I saw his rendering for some of the rides. Instead of horses, the merry-go-round has riders sitting on toilet seats that go up and down.

FUN FACT

Kenny Irwin's motto is, "Cats were made to meow. I was made to make art."

Kenny Irwin (Photograph by Henry Lehn)

✳ JUMPING CACTI?

Palm Springs is filled with jumping cacti, so don't get too close to one. Native to the Sonoran Desert, its official name is cylindropuntia fulgida. The shrub's barbed cactus spikes don't actually jump. They do, however, easily detach from the main plant and hook tenaciously into you. While taking this photo, I got too close. Several spikes penetrated my shoe and went into my foot. Keep pets away. My dog got too close and had to go to an emergency vet clinic.

- Robolights -

Rock Houses
Indian Canyons & Araby Cove

This camouflaged rock house in Indian Canyons comes with a stone balcony.

Palm Springs has had no shortage of visionary architects. Yet an architect we hear little about and never celebrate is R. Lee Miller, who in the 1920s built secretive houses here out of rocks and boulders that are disguised to blend into their untamed surroundings. Informally trained, Miller liked to camouflage his houses, building in very difficult places such as the sides of mountains. Rare photos show he didn't resemble a Bohemian artist but the ruggedly handsome sportswear type. Think Errol Flynn. Miller was also friends with Cabot Yerxa, whose rock house in Desert Hot Springs is now the Cabot Pueblo Museum. The two most dramatic of Lee's developments are in Andreas Canyon and Araby Cove.

Andreas Canyon Club

There are 22 rock houses in this hidden community. You can see some of them from Andreas Canyon. They are at the end of the half-mile streamside hiking trail, which starts at the parking lot. They are kept safe from trespassers by a metal fence and signs that say "Andreas Canyon Club" and "No Trespassing." The Club was formed in 1921 by conservation-minded Los Angeles businessmen who bought this property from the Southern Pacific Railroad. Walt Disney wanted to be a member but was turned down because of the attention he would bring. The entrance is via an unmarked gated road off South Palm Canyon Drive, not far from the kiosk entrance to Andreas Canyon.

Araby Cove

Three rock houses were built in Araby Cove.

There are five of Miller's rock houses — or what's left of them — on 20 acres just above the Palm Canyon Wash. They were designed to be a Hopi village. Don't let the structures deceive you. Although they look squat and demure, they are built like bunkers with steps leading down to the front doors. There's even an Olympic-size pool, now abandoned. Exteriors and interiors feature native rock and handcrafted everything: doors, windows, shelves and iron door latches. The floors are a kaleidoscope of green, yellow, pink and blue rock. Masonry around the houses is stamped with Hopi designs. Miller called this compound Indian Village and lived there for many years.

The main houses have been occupied by various kinds of owners: artists, cowgirls, gun-toting socialites and a society hairdresser. One of the now-dilapidated cottages was named Casa Contenta. One woman — not so contenta — said she moved out because her house became infested with scorpions. The main Round House is now a vacation rental. The other four huts are pretty much in ruins.

SIGHTSEEING TIP: " You can best see these three rock house by looking down at them from Araby Road, but to do that you risk venturing onto private property and streets. Better to see them with binoculars from the northern bank of the Palm Canyon Wash, where Barona Road ends (see: Araby Cove/Palm Canyon Wash)."

FACT CHECKING: A Palm Springs myth says the Araby Cove rock houses were built as a getaway for the actors who played the Munchkins in the "The Wizard of Oz." That couldn't be, as that movie came out in 1939.

- Rock Houses -

Royal Hawaiian Estates

1774 South Palm Canyon Drive, South Palm Springs

After World War II, California went Polynesia crazy. Directly across from the Moorten Botanical Garden on South Palm Canyon Drive is the Royal Hawaiian Estates, Palm Springs's first tiki-themed condo complex. Built in 1961 and designed by Donald Wexler and Richard Harrison, it blends their modernist aesthetic with Polynesian architectural detailing, lush gardens, carved tiki statuary and "tiki apexes," which are triangular forms that are found at the end of beams and that emulate a sailing ship's riggings. Although condos are standard two- or three- bedroom units, they are hardly standard. They feature walls of glass in every room that open onto large private patios with views of Diamond Head — OK, the San Jacinto Mountains. In 2010, the complex became the city of Palm Springs's first residential historic district.

- Royal Hawaiian Estates -

Ruth Hardy Park
700 Tamarisk Road, Movie Colony

Mayor Charles Farrell and Ruth Hardy at a city council meeting. (Photograph courtesy of the Palm Springs Historical Society - All Rights Reserved)

Ruth Hardy Park comes with a palm tree oasis that has resting benches.

Ruth Hardy Park is in the heart of the Movie Colony. Its 22 acres are encompassed by Tamarisk Road, Tacheva Drive, Via Miraleste and Avenida Caballeros. In fall 2005 it was rechristened Wellness Park, though it's still mostly known as Ruth Hardy Park. The park's expansive green lawns, shade trees and flower gardens separate the Movie Colony from the newer Movie Colony East. The park has tennis, volleyball and basketball courts, weight-bearing exercise stations, picnic tables and grills. Need to chill from too much sightseeing? There are meditation paths that you can wander. You can bring your dog here, too, on a leash.

Ruth Hardy was one of Palm Springs's visionary pioneer women who owned and ran the Ingleside Inn in the Historic Tennis District (see: Ingleside Inn). She became the first woman to be elected to the city council, in 1948. Her achievements include getting streetlights banned in most neighborhoods to protect the night sky, commercial signs forbidden above storefronts, and the planting and lighting of palm trees along Palm Canyon Drive, which began in 1947 at the cost of $1 million that she raised. As the village grew, she wanted to make sure it would always retain its resort-oriented allure. She died in 1965 at age 73 and is interred in the Wellwood Murray Memorial Cemetery.

SAFETY TIP: When walking at night, carry a flashlight or wear a head lamp, and don't bicycle after sundown.

- Ruth Hardy Park -

What to SEE in Palm Springs

Saint Theresa of the Child Jesus Church

2800 Ramon Road, Midtown

Most tourists drive right past Saint Theresa Church on Ramon Road. It's easy to miss the Catholic church, as much of it is surrounded by a stylized granite wall. When I have visitors, I take them there. It's a mid-century gem.

Built in 1968, Saint Theresa's is considered mid-century architect William F. Cody's masterwork. He wanted it to be different from any other Catholic church, and it is — but only in its design, which resembles a Japanese temple. Saint Theresa's incorporates aspects of mid-century architecture, such as floor-to-ceiling windows and clerestory windows. Like many modernists, Cody embraced the Eastern notion of "less is more." The wall provides private areas where people can pray and meditate. The wall blocks sunlight, creating a sense of spiritual separation, a holy place where one could forget the outside world. Felled by a stroke in 1971, he died in 1978 at age 62

As you walk down the center aisle of the church toward the altar, the ceiling swoops upward to a dramatic apex. To achieve cohesiveness, Cody worked on every detail of the church. He even designed its abstract stained-glass windows and picked out the Italian glass. One reason he took such care is he was a member of the congregation. It's also where Bob and Dolores Hope worshiped. In January 1998, it was the site of Sonny Bono's funeral.

- Saint Theresa of the Child Jesus Church -

Sammy Davis Jr.'s House
444 Chino Drive, Cemetery District

Singer/dancer/actor Sammy Davis Jr. was a force, a swizzle stick in the cocktail of life. Just after marrying his third and last wife, the late Altovise Gore, in 1970, he moved into this nondescript house across from Temple Isaiah. The super-energetic, 5-foot-6, 120-pound Rat Packer was known, like Frank Sinatra, to be extremely generous, always ready to perform at a charity event here. He was an avid golfer, one of the first members of the Tamarisk Country Club in Rancho Mirage. Unlike other Coachella Valley golf resorts, Tamarisk membership was open to celebrities, Jews and minorities. Davis checked all boxes. Surprisingly, there' isn't a street here named after him.

PERSONAL NOTE: I was lucky to have interviewed Sammy Davis Jr. one late night in his dressing room at Harrah's Reno. He didn't want to do the interview but eventually relented, and after it was over, invited me to stay for a drink. I can't recall how many drinks we had or what we talked about. I do remember him playing a joke on me. As I was leaving his dressing room, he gave me a big Sammy Davis Jr. embrace, then suddenly pulled away. "Sorry, man, I shouldn't be hugging people, it gets me in trouble," he said. "How so?" I asked, taking the bait. "When I was in China, I tried to hug Mao Tse Tung, but his bodyguard stopped me, saying, 'Mr. Davis, please don't squeeze the Chairman.'" With that corny Mr. Whipple joke, Davis doubled over with laughter and hugged me again. (The full story is at johnrstark.net.)

FACT CHECKING: A local story says that after Sammy Davis Jr. died in 1990, his widow, Altovise, couldn't pay the mortgage on this house. So, she had Sammy's body disinterred at Forest Lawn Memorial Park in L.A., then sold the jewelry that was on him, including a diamond watch, which allowed her to pay off the property. When I asked a friend of the late Altovise about this, she replied, "Never, ever happened!"

- Sammy Davis Jr. House -

San Gorgonio Pass Wind Farm
North Palm Springs

Best seen on the west side of Indian Canyon Drive heading to Desert Hot Springs.

The San Gorgonio Pass wind farm stretches all the way from the eastern slope of the San Gorgonio Pass, near Cabazon, to North Palm Springs. This is the world's first wind farm. You know you're arriving in the Coachella Valley from Los Angeles when you see out your car window some 2,700 white steel towers on the desert sand and hillsides, many 300 feet high. They are as arresting as any Christo environmental installation, whirling dervishes receiving the wind's beneficence. Electrifying us. We didn't always love them, though. In 1985, the City of Palm Springs sued the Bureau of Land Management to halt further development. The city claimed they were a blight on the desert landscape, blocking mountain views and threatening tourism. The winds of public opinion have certainly changed. Today, these images are on the cover of our promotional brochures.

The San Gorgonio corridor is one of the windiest spots on the planet, as anyone who has flown in or out of Palm Springs can tell you. In this narrow pass, hot desert air collides with moist, cooler temperatures that create wind funnels. With the artistry of a pastry chef, these wind funnels create delicate sand dunes, which are called aeolian sand dunes. When the winds are really blowing, waves of aeolian sand dunes crash over Indian Canyon Drive and Gene Autry Trail, closing them to traffic. (A major concern about building a bridge over the dunes is protection of the endangered Casey's June beetle, a unique species whose natural habitat is in those sands.)

Today, these windmills annually generate some 1.5 million kilowatt hours of electricity. Most of that turbine power goes to Los Angeles. It isn't only wind that makes these turbines spin. It's money. Owners sell their electricity to Southern California Edison, which then distributes it. Most of the windmills are privately owned. A single turbine can cost many millions of dollars.

Wind turbines work on a simple principle: Instead of using electricity to make wind, wind turbines use wind to make electricity. Wind turns the propellor-like blades of a turbine around a rotor, which spins a generator, which in turn creates electricity. Upwind turbines, like the ones here, face into the wind, while

(Photograph by Henry Lehn)

downwind turbines face away. The lifespan of a wind turbine is 25 to 30 years. The older ones from the 1980s and 1990s are being replaced with bigger, more powerful ones. As time goes on, there are fewer of them. Made of steel, the new white ones are some 26 stories high with foot-

ball-field-length blades. When winds reach 55 mph, the newer ones shut down, whereas the older ones shut down when the wind reaches 35 mph.

Businessmen may only see the windmills as money generators. Many, however, see them as backdrops. Countless Instagram photos depict young folks doing cartwheels in front of them. The windmills are most alluring when backlit by the setting sun. One of the best places to see them at that time is on North Indian Canyon Drive heading towards Interstate 10 and Desert Hot Springs. If you want a really close-up look, you can park and get out of your car at the Amtrak station on Palm Springs Station Road.

FUN FACT

Desert Hot Springs was nicknamed Desperate Hot Springs after declaring bankruptcy in 2004. That moniker got dropped after it became the first city in California to legalize the cultivation of pot. Land that is zoned for cultivation is now going for up to a million dollars an acre. Desert Hot Springs now promotes itself as "The Napa Valley of Cannabis." With more than 30 marijuana outlets in Palm Springs, we've been nicknamed Pot Springs.

- San Gorgonio Pass Wind Farm -

UN-FUN FACT

Two Bunch Palms, the exclusive Desert Hot Springs spa, was used in the 1920s by mobster Al Capone as his hideaway. My Palm Springs neighbor, Chris, who grew up here, told me that a detective he knew once told him: "If they could dig up all the murdered bodies that are buried between Palm Springs and Desert Hot Springs and stand them straight up, you wouldn't have a desert. You'd have a forest."

detour

MARIJUANA AND DATE SHAKES

Continuing on Indian Canyon Drive heading north, you'll pass a large beetle bug on your left, just before crossing over Interstate 10 (See: Hole in the Wall). Once over the overpass of the Sonny Bono Memorial Freeway, you're in **Desert Hot Springs**. On the right side of the highway, you'll pass Coachillin', a 160-acre "canna-business park" that's under development. When completed it will feature three million square feet of cultivation, manufacturing, processing, testing, distribution, touring and education facilities. Planned is a hotel, restaurants, private club, retail stores and an amphitheater with seating for 5,000. To the east of Coachillin' is Mike Tyson's proposed Tyson Ranch, a deluxe cannabis resort. Beyond that at the intersection of Dillon Road is the funky Windmill Market, where locals go for Medjool date shakes. I am always taking out-of-town guests there for an off-the-tourist-path experience. Closed Sundays.

- San Gorgonio Pass Wind Farm -

Sandcliff

1800 Barona Road, South Palm Springs

Should you ring a doorbell at the Sandcliff condominium complex on Barona Road, don't be surprised if Laura Petrie answers in Capri pants. Or sporting a Catalina bathing suit with a flowered swim cap on her way for a dip in one of the three, David Hockney-blue swimming pools. Built in 1964, Sandcliff was one of the prototypes for the "lifestyle" complexes that became so popular throughout Palm Springs. So much so that in 2015, the Palm Springs Historic Site Preservation Board designated Sandcliff a historic district. Interiors on some of these 40 units retain their original all-electric kitchens, sliding draw stovetops, intercom wall systems and popcorn ceilings.

- Sandcliff -

Santorini House
400 West Camino Alturas, The Mesa

The architect for the strikingly unusual Santorini House was William Nicholson, who also designed the controversial Flintstone house in Hillsborough, Calif., which people yabba-dabba-do love or yabba-dabba-don't. Same goes for the Santorini, which was also built in the 1970s. Some 45 years later, it was redesigned as an Antoni Gaudi-like Greek-style villa. To achieve its bulbous shape, concrete was put over inflated weather balloons. An outdoor spiral staircase leads from the swimming pool area to a domed rooftop patio. Best way to see the house is to take West El Portal off South Palm Canyon Drive until it ends. Take caution backing up and turning around.

- Santorini House -

Section 14 Indian Sculptures
Midtown

These striking bronze sculptures mark the southwest and southeast borders of Section 14 (aka Area 14), a one square mile of tribal land in the heart of downtown. The women with the basket and water jug are on the dividing strip of East Tahquitz Canyon Way at North Indian Canyon Drive across from the Agua Caliente Cultural Plaza. The sculpture depicting a native family is on the dividing strip of East Tahquitz Canyon Way near Sunrise Way. Both are by artist Doug Hyde, who is of Nez Perce, Assiniboine and Chippewa descent.

Located in Section 14 is the hot springs, the Agua Caliente Cultural Plaza, the Agua Caliente Casino, the Convention Center, Living Out (a nine-acre, LGBTQ 55-plus living complex) and the U.S. Post Office. Alongside gated condo complexes you'll see yet-to-be-developed scrub land, which is home to many a jackrabbit, roadrunner and coyote.

- Section 14 Indian Sculptures -

✳ HOT BED OF CONTROVERSY

Until the early 1960s, Section 14 was inhabited by domestics, gardeners, laborers and service workers. In those days, Palm Springs was comprised largely of the haves and the have-nots who worked for them. While the west side of Indian Canyon Drive was white and wealthy, Section 14 was a land of substandard houses, trailers and shacks in plain sight of tourists. Because Section 14 is on tribal land, it generated no property taxes. The City, therefore, would not provide services, including water, electricity and sewage. Until 1955, federal laws prevented the Agua Caliente Indians from leasing their land for longer than five years at a time, thus inhibiting investment in infrastructure and making obtaining mortgages impossible. In 1959, the federal government expanded tribal lease rights to 99 years. Section 14 was now primed for massive development, and property values soared. To protect Indians who wanted to sell their lands from being ripped off, the federal government required them to have conservators. This led to all kinds of trickery by judges and lawyers.

In 1962, the city of Palm Springs began clearing lots to make way for development, displacing some 200 residents. Although the city reportedly issued three-year eviction notices, some say they never received them and came home from work to find their houses bulldozed. In the summer of 2022, lawsuits were filed against the city for financial compensation to former residents and their descendants. City documents do show that the city acted at the request of the tribal owners of the land, who wanted to exercise their newly granted right to develop it.

- Section 14 Indian Sculptures -

ALL WOMAN TRIBAL COUNCIL

The year 1954 saw the first all-woman Tribal Council of the Agua Caliente Band of Cahuilla Indians. It was, in fact, the first all-woman tribal council in America. Chairperson Vyola J. Ortner traveled regularly to Washington, DC and Sacramento to lobby for the General Leasing Act of 1959, authorized by Congress and signed by President Dwight Eisenhower. This was the historic act that provided 99-year leases on Agua Caliente tribal lands. Ortner, who died in 2017 at age 95, was on the front lines of many important issues that faced the tribe at a time when members were subjected to egregious treatment and outdated government regulations. She and the all-woman Tribal Council helped shape a modern reservation and Palm Springs. You can read about her life and accomplishments in her biography, "You Can't Eat Dirt." It's a great read that's packed with historical photos. Available at our public library.

BABY, IT'S YOU

Although an 1891 federal law gave allotment of the Agua Caliente reservation land to individual tribe members, this process didn't begin happening until 1959. This followed decades of legal battles. The tribe decided to give the first choice of parcels to its youngest and poorest member, Steven Rice, born in Banning, California, on Aug. 13 1958. The AP photograph of 2-year-old Steve Rice collecting $325,000 worth of Palm Springs real estate went national.

A LINK TO LINDBERGH

In 1930, a small commercial airport was built in Section 14. The first plane to land there was the sister ship to Charles Lindbergh's Spirit of St. Louis. Some remains of those runways still exist.

- Section 14 Indian Sculptures -

Ship of the Desert House
1995 South Camino Monte, The Mesa

This is a historically protected, 4,400-square-foot residence that resembles an Art Deco ocean liner. You half expect to see the Duke and Duchess of Windsor waving to you from its curved redwood deck, gin and tonics in hand. Sunset magazine christened the hillside manor "the Ship of the Desert" when it was completed in 1937, and the name stuck. It was immediately hailed as revolutionary for its streamline moderne style of architecture. If you lived in Palm Springs in the 1920s and '30s, and had money, you built a Moroccan/Spanish villa. This house forever changed the look of Palm Springs as it inspired architects to break from tradition.

In 1998, fashion designer Trina Turk and her photographer husband, the late Jonathan Skow, bought the fabled landmark. A mysterious fire broke out while work was being done on it, destroying 75% of the interior. The devastated but determined couple rebuilt, recreating the original in almost every detail.

"Good times and bum times, I've seen them all/And, my dear, I'm still here."

--Stephen Sondheim

- Ship of the Desert House -

Shiprock & Angel Cove
North Palm Springs

If you take the first Palm Springs exit off Interstate 10 heading east, you'll find yourself on Highway 111. Shortly before reaching the Palm Springs Visitors Center, you'll pass two landmarks sporting historical plaques that say "Shiprock" and "Angel Cove."

Shiprock is a rock formation that bears a likeness to a Spanish galleon, thus its name. Geologists say Shiprock was formed during the late Paleozoic Era when layers of silt and decaying sea organisms were laid down, compressed, heated and slowly moved northward for thousands of miles along the west side of the San Andreas Fault. In the process, the rock was uplifted, tilted and exposed by the up-thrusting granite of Mount San Jacinto. The Cahuilla Indians, who have lived here for more than 5,000 years, call Shiprock kista cavel, which means "sharp pointed rocks." There's a small parking area alongside the highway and a walking path around the rock.

Angel Cove is a scenic and wildlife habitat, which has a small parking area that abuts Shiprock. High on the mountain is a rock cluster that is lighter than the surrounding terrain. This formation resembles an angel with "wings" on both sides, depending on the time of day. I've yet to see it; maybe you'll be lucky. There's a myth that the formation wasn't named for any resemblance to a heavenly being. A long-ago settler of the cove believed that an angel saved her sick child. The Friends of the Palm Springs Mountains were the angels who saved this area from development. The land was donated to the City of Palm Springs in 2017.

TAKE NOTE: If you're driving north on Highway 111 to see Shiprock and Angel Cove, you can only cross the highway at the Whitewater turnoff a mile down the road. There's only a small sign, so keep an eye out for it.

FACT CHECKING: There's a myth that ancient ships, such as Spanish galleons, are buried in the lower Sonoran Desert. While it's true that the desert was once a tropical ocean, that was 250 million years ago.

- Shiprock & Angel Cove -

Smoke Tree Ranch

1850 Smoke Tree Lane, South Palm Springs

The guarded entrance to Smoke Tree Ranch.

Smoke Tree Ranch is one of Palm Springs's most exclusive areas to live, even though it lacks Spanish villas and McMansions. You can see the guardhouse and gate leading into the community from Smoke Tree Lane, which cuts through the center of the Smoke Tree Commons shopping complex on East Palm Canyon Drive. Smoke Tree Ranch has 85 modest houses on its 375 secluded acres. Street names and addresses are written on boulders. Houses rarely go on sale. If they do, they aren't advertised. Open houses and for sale signs are forbidden.

Smoke Tree Ranch was a working ranch until its owners transformed it into a colony of houses in 1936. Smoke Tree Ranch did not advertise or seek publicity. It appealed to a cosmopolitan group who shared the "Smoke Tree way of life," according to the website. Envisioned was a place where "free from pressures, like-minded people, with their families, could enjoy the desert." Many of these "like-minded" colonists were originally Los Angeles executives who wanted a break from their high-pressure jobs. Here they could play cowboy and cowgirl.

Celebrities weren't allowed to buy here, although in 1948 Walt Disney charmed his way in. So, too, did Tennessee Ernie Ford. When Disney decided to build Disneyland, he asked the other residents if they would like to in-

- Smoke Tree Ranch -

vest. No takers. In 1954, he sold his house to raise money for his theme park. A much wealthier Disney did mosey back to Smoke Tree Ranch in 1957 and bought two houses. His return was welcomed until he tried to put a railroad train around one of the houses. "Whoa!" the board of directors said, "you're not that charming."

From Barona Road you can peek into secluded Smoke Tree Ranch.

President Eisenhower turned Smoke Tree Ranch into a Western White House for several days in 1954. It was Ike's first visit to the Coachella Valley, where he retired. Historical photos show him enjoying cookouts with the residents. The centerpiece of the Smoke Tree Ranch is the ranch house and dining hall. Every evening, a dinner bell is rung – a tradition from the old days. Colonists are treated to three full meals a day that's paid for by their HOA dues. Other amenities include a riding stable and tennis club. If you don't know any colonists to bunk with, you might be in luck. You can rent one of Smoke Tree's 49 cottages that are near the stables. They do, however, book up years in advance. They aren't cheap, so bring plenty of silver dollars.

SIGHTSEEING TIP: The best insider view of Smoke Tree Ranch is from atop the Palm Canyon Wash levee at the end of Barona Road in South Palm Springs. Walking westward along the levee you'll look down into it.

FUN FACT

At one time, Walt Disney considered putting Disneyland in Thousand Palms, east of Palm Springs. Talk about a Mickey Mouse move. Who would stand in line to ride Dumbo when temps are in the triple digits?

- Smoke Tree Ranch -

SMOKE TREE STABLES

The Smoke Tree Ranch stables offer public horse-back rides to the Santa Rosa Mountains, and to Andreas and Murray canyons. The stables are located at 2500 South Toledo Avenue, where South Toledo and East Murray Canyon Drive intersect. Check out their website: www.smoketreestables.com.

SMOKE TREE BUSH

Smoke trees aren't trees but shrubs. They are arboreal magicians that look from a distance like plumes of smoke. This illusion has to do with their gray-colored leaves, grey-green branches and wavy looking trunks. Put these elements together and you have created desert sorcery. Smoke trees are indigenous to the southwest, loving heat and extreme direct sunlight. In early summer months, smoke trees perform another magic trick, exploding in a magnificent bloom of blue to violet flowers. You don't have to go to a wash or arroyo to find them. Used in landscaping, they are plentiful in the Smoke Tree Commons shopping area on East Palm Canyon Drive and near the Smoke Tree stables on Murray Canyon Drive in Indian Canyons.

IKE & THE UFO?

On March 20, 1954, while staying at Smoke Tree Ranch, President Dwight Eisenhower mysteriously disappeared for a day. The AP reported he'd died but quickly retracted this statement. Considering Ike's stiff demeanor, it's easy to see how that mistake got made. Ike did disappear. It's believed he went to "a nearby air force base" to see a dentist, having chipped a tooth while eating grilled chicken at a Smoke Tree Ranch cookout. Conspiracy theories claim the dentist story was a cover for what really happened: Ike had a secret desert rendezvous with extraterrestrials. Through mental telepathy, the aliens were able to tell him why they came to Planet Earth and, unlike the Purple People Eater, it wasn't to get a job in a rock 'n' roll band. They wanted the U.S. to eliminate its nuclear weapons before the universe suffered irreparable damage.

- Smoke Tree Ranch -

Sonny Bono Sculpture
155 South Palm Canyon Drive, Downtown

The bronze sculpture of Sonny Bono at the Mercado Plaza downtown at South Palm Canyon Drive depicts the entertainer-turned-politician sitting on the edge of a water fountain. He appears to be welcoming visitors to downtown, an appropriate gesture as he was instrumental in revitalizing Palm Springs's economy during his term as mayor from 1988 to 1992. Installed in 2001, the sculpture is by Russian-American artist Emmanuil Snitkovsky, who also did the nearby Lucy Ricardo Bench sculpture. Notice how shiny Bono's thighs are from so many tourists sitting on his lap to have their photos taken. Most don't sit for long. They quickly jump off; copper gets very hot under the desert sun. That may explain Sonny's sly grin. He got you, babe!

Bono and his fourth wife, Mary, moved to Palm Springs from Los Angeles in 1986. He was 51 and had been divorced from Cher for 11 years. They bought an estate in The Mesa area next to Suzanne Somers's villa and opened a restaurant on North Indian Canyon Drive. Sonny claimed the restaurant's short life span was due to bureaucracy at City Hall. He said City Hall was run by special real estate and development interests. Sonny, determined to make things easier for businesses, ran for mayor in 1988 and defeated six other candidates in a landslide. When his term ended, he was elected to the U.S. House of Representatives for the 44th district here. In 1998, he died in a skiing accident at Lake Tahoe. Mary succeeded him in office.

Bono is credited as being the driving force behind the Palm Springs International Film Festival, which began in 1990 and is held every January at the Convention Center. With his connections, he helped give Palm Springs back its celebrity clout.

- Sonny Bono Sculpture -

On July 31, 1991, Bono faced the hardest day of his life: A bus filled with girl scouts coming back from a trip up the Palm Springs Aerial Tramway lost control on Tramway Road. Six scouts and the bus driver were killed and 47 others, including chaperones, were injured. As soon as Bono heard the news, he rushed to the scene. He helped carry backboards bearing injured riders up rugged terrain to ambulances and helicopters.

Perhaps Bono's biggest legacy is that he reined in spring break. In 1986, 80 spring breakers were arrested. Downtown was party central. Sacred Tahquitz Canyon was trashed by campers. Store windows were being smashed and businesses looted. Baton-waving riot police saturated the warm night air with tear gas. Downtown traffic was at a standstill as cars filled with young revelers made a loop around Palm Canyon and Indian Canyon drives. Bono came up with some creative ways to take the spring out of spring break:

* Indian Canyon Drive was made one way running south to north to prevent cars from driving in a loop. This kept spring beakers from stopping and conversing with each other. In 2022 Indian Canyon was made two-way again.
* To further help keep the teens away, loudspeakers were placed downtown blasting opera music at night.
* To even further keep revelers away, thongs and bikinis were banned downtown. That ordinance had to be repealed as no one was coming downtown.

In remembrance of Bono:

* The Salton Sea National Wildlife Refuge was renamed the Sonny Bono Salton Sea National Wildlife Refuge.
* The open-air, terminal concourse at the Palm Springs International Airport is named after him.
* A 40-mile stretch of Interstate 10 bears his name.

detour

Sonny is buried in Desert Park Memorial cemetery, which is at the corner of Ramon Road and Da Vall Drive in Cathedral City. His remains are in Row B-35, Plot 294.

- Sonny Bono Sculpture -

Street Marker
Uptown District

This is one of the last remaining stone street markers in Palm Springs. It was erected in 1938 just after the city was incorporated. Back then, Palm Canyon Drive was Palm Canyon Boulevard; before that, it was Main Street. The marker is on the corner of West Chino Drive and North Palm Canyon Drive.

- Street Marker -

Sunmor Estates
City Hall/Airport

Newly renovated Sunmor mod-pod.

Tucked behind City Hall is Sunmor Estates. You'll see the sign for the entrance to the retro neighborhood at Farrell Drive and Livmor Avenue, a block or so north of Tahquitz Canyon Drive. The model home, bearing a plaque, is at 2821 Livmor. The house above is on Plaimor.

Sunmor is a remarkably intact collection of mid-century modern houses. Don Draper couldn't have marketed them any better. "Enchanted homes," the brochures said. Street names are a play on words that evoke suburban bliss: Morsun, Livmor, Easmor and Plaimor. Palm Springs's cowboy mayor, Frank Bogert, lived at 2787 East Plaimor Ave., giving the enclave panache.

Built in the mid-to-late 1950s, the single-family post-and-beam houses are about 1,350 square feet, have carports (or did) and originally sold for $17,500. Although Twin Palms Estates is credited as being Palm Springs's first modernist tract development, Sunmor is a very close second, if not tied. Unlike Twin Palms Estates,

- Sunmor Estates -

these houses didn't come with swimming pools. Pools were special-order. Unlike Twin Palms Estates, they did come with air conditioning. Many in this subdivision have been refurbished back to their original coolness. Check out those long slanted rooflines, as sexy as slingback kitten heels.

The enclave was designed by desert architects Donald Wexler and Richard Harrison and built, at least in the beginning, by developer Bob Higgins. After 1957, it was completed by William Krisel and the Alexander Construction Company. This change took place after 11 of the 45 houses were completed. Stories vary as to what happened. Two cul-de-sacs are named after members of the Alexander family, Helena and Jill circles. If you want more Sunmor, there's an extension of the neighborhood on East Juanita Drive off Farrell Drive. Sunmor is a designated Class 1 Historic Neighborhood.

✳ HISTORIC TIE-DOWNS

The concrete circle on Easmor is also a protected Class 1 historic site. During World War II, this area was a military base and airfield. Unlike the coast, the clear desert air almost always allowed for takeoffs and landings. Military aircraft of every type were stored here, on high alert for a Japanese attack. The U.S. Army Corps of Engineers built the circles, which are called tie-downs or hardstand circles. The planes at night were secured by fasteners so that no one could steal them. The planes were serviced, inspected and by morning dispersed to allied bases around the world. Notice that the east end of Sunmor has a street called Airplane Drive.

- Sunmor Estates -

Sunny Dunes Vintage District
East Sunny Dunes Road

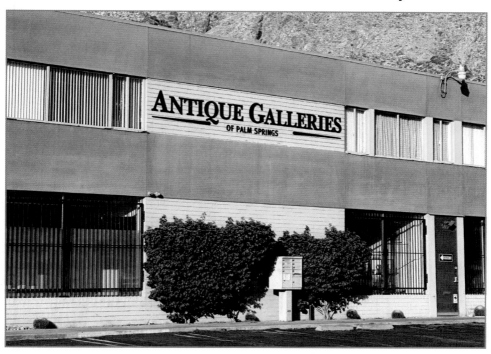

Of the dozen or so antique stores in this industrial area of southwest Palm Springs — AKA the Vintage District — the most visible is the ocean -liner sized Sunny Dunes Antique Mall. If you're into fine porcelain, old dolls or Victoriana, this is neither the store nor the neighborhood to visit. If you are into vintage mid-century, have at it, from Eames chairs to lazy susans. The Vintage District includes Builders Supply hardware Store and the Tool Shed, a gay bar also known for its vintage treasures. This clandestine cluster of antique, vintage, art, and thrift stores are open most days 10 a.m. to 5 p.m.

- Sunny Dunes Vintage District -

Sunrise Park
Midtown

In the very center of Palm Springs, across the street from Ralph's supermarket on Sunrise Way, is Sunrise Park, which until the mid-1970s was a polo ground. Its 38 acres include the Mizell Center for seniors, public library, baseball stadium, skateboard park, swim center and pavilion dance hall/leisure center. Sunrise Park has outdoor picnic tables, grills and play structures. Every first Sunday in April you can experience Opera in the Park, which features a stage full of opera singers and musicians. And its free. Called "Wave Rhythms," this wind-driven, red and black  stainless-steel sculpture by local artist John Mishler is prominent on North Sunrise Way. The metal sculpture of the hawk, sheep and coyote is located at the entrance to the pavilion. At right, local school students cool off and get exercise by playing water polo at the Swim Center.

- Sunrise Park -

PALM SPRINGS STADIUM
1901 E. Baristo Road

The Palm Springs Stadium in **Sunrise Park** is home to the Power Baseball team and the California Winter League. The Power team recruits elite collegiate players from around the country to come to Palm Springs and play baseball in the sweltering hot months of June and July. The California Winter League operates every January and February. It features pro free agent baseball players trying to earn a spot to a pro roster before the start of spring training.

At the stadium's entrance is an abstract sculpture of baseball players at bat.

- Sunrise Park -

Swiss Miss Houses
New Las Palmas

When in 1962 architects William Krisel and Dan Saxon Palmer decided to develop Vista Las Palmas, a tract development of 330 houses, buyers wanted a roof design that they could call their own. After all, Twin Palms Estates, which Alexander Construction and Krisel had just developed, made the butterfly roof iconic to that neighborhood and eventually to all of Palm Springs. What came to be in Vista Las Palmas were A-frames called Swiss Misses. These are low-lying one-story residences that have dramatic, A-frame roofs that rise straight from the ground. Krisel found the fusion design tacky; in fact, when he was asked in later years who came up with that concept, he blew up and said, "Some damn fool in the office!" Krisel and Palmer's firm appointed architect Charles DuBois to execute the Swiss Misses, which proved a hit with buyers. DuBois had spent a good deal of time in Hawaii, which is probably where he got the inspiration for them. Luau or fondue party? This is California. You can do both.

- Swiss Miss Houses -

What to SEE in Palm Springs

Tahquitz Canyon
500 West Mesquite Avenue, West Palm Springs

Tahquitz Canyon Visitor's Center

Many sites in Palm Springs are worth getting out of your car to see and explore; Tahquitz Canyon being one. To get there, drive to the very end of Mesquite Avenue heading west. At the foot of the mountains, you'll come to the Agua Caliente visitor's center and trading post. This is the gateway to Tahquitz Canyon, named after what the Tahquitz call Nukatem ("sacred being"). Pay an entrance fee and you can take a two-mile roundtrip hike through the narrow canyon, home to rock art, ancient irrigation systems, native plants, wildlife and at the end the big reveal: a spectacular 60-foot waterfall. The trail is mostly flat but does require stepping up and down over rocks and occasional boulders. The Indians will lend you a hand-carved walking stick to keep you balanced. Best to go in the cooler months,

The 60-foot Tahquitz Falls.

especially in spring when the snowmelt from the mountains add to the waterfall's velocity. Best to go early in the day as the afternoon sun reflecting off the canyon walls can be harsh. You are required to bring water, which you can buy at the trading post.

- Tahquitz Canyon -

✳ HERMIT OF TAHQUITZ CANYON

The Hermit of Tahquitz Canyon - William Pester. (Photograph courtesy of the
Palm Springs Historical Society, All Rights Reserved)

The fabled "Hermit of Tahquitz Canyon" was German immigrant
William Pester who came to Palm Springs in 1916 at age 31. He
embraced a German-Swiss social movement called lebensre-
form, which advocated a back-to-nature lifestyle. Pester found
his paradise in the secluded Tahquitz Canyon, where he built a
shack. He embraced nudism, lived on raw fruits and vegetables,
and became a respected friend of the Indians. Tourists flocked to
Tahquitz Canyon in their Model Ts to get a look at him. Celebrities
like Charlie Chaplin embraced him. Rudolph Valentino did more
than that, staying with him when he was in town. In 1940, Pester's paradise became hell when he was arrested for having sex
with a male minor. Labeled a sexual pervert, he spent six years
in San Quentin and Folsom state prisons. After being paroled,
Pester settled in Los Angeles, got married and died in Arizona in
1973 at age 88.

He lives on in song: In 1948, Nat King Cole had his first solo
hit (on Capitol Records), "Nature Boy," about Pester. The jazz
ballad's melody and lyrics were by eden ahbez, who spelled his
name lower case. A Los Angeles naturalist, he lived under the
first "L" in the Hollywood sign. He considered Pester his mentor.
"Nature Boy" has been covered by an aviary of songbirds, from
Sarah Vaughn to Lady Gaga, and is the theme song of Baz Luhr-
man's "Moulin Rouge". No one knows if Pester and ahbetz ever
met; ahbetz died in 1995 at age 87.

*"The greatest thing you'll ever learn, is just to love
and be loved in return." – "Nature Boy"*

- Tahquitz Canyon -

PARADISE FOUND

Director Frank Capra said he found paradise when he first saw Tahquitz Canyon. He used the falls in his 1937 film "Lost Horizon," based on James Hilton's novel about a Himalayan village called Shangri-La — where, much like Palm Springs, no one ages as long as they don't leave. The film starred Ronald Coleman, Jane Wyatt and a beautiful young actress named Margo; easier to fit on a marquee than her birth name, Maria Marguerita Guadalupe Teresa Estela Bolado Castilla y O'Donnell. Capra filmed a scene of a horse and rider atop Tahquitz Falls. The horse had to be airlifted to the top of the cataract with a winch.

 ## PARADISE LOST

In 1969, the city and four law enforcement agencies cleared Tahquitz Canyon of hippies who had encamped there and trashed the sacred grounds.

 ## THE WITCH OF TAHQUITZ CANYON

If you look at the entrance to Tahquitz Canyon in the morning hours of mid-summer, fall and winter, you'll see the Witch of Tahquitz Canyon. The shadowy figure can be seen making daily flights on her broomstick, black cape flowing in the wind. Some say the witch isn't a "she" or "he" but a gender-neutral shaman. Others say the witch is a shadow, nothing more. The clearest view of the Witch of Tahquitz Canyon occurs at the intersection of Hermosa Drive and Amado Road. Farrell Drive, just south of Vista Chino, is an excellent place to witch-spot, too.

- Tahquitz Canyon -

✳ SHEEP THRILLS

The bighorn sheep that live in our rugged canyons and along our steep mountainsides originally came across the Bering land bridge from Siberia into Alaska 750,000 years ago. Good places to spot them in Palm Springs are Tahquitz, Andreas and Chino canyons. Even though bighorns keep daylight hours, sightings are rare, which makes coming upon one even more special. There are about 100 bighorns in our foothills; in 1998 they were awarded federal endangered species protection, so populations are slowly coming

(Photograph by Henry Lehn)

back. They move quietly, not announcing themselves. Standing still against rock formations they could be petroglyphs painted by local cavemen. As you're walking along a canyon trail you may hear a scuffle from above that's followed by loose rocks. Look up. Standing on a narrow ledge or stony outcropping will be a bighorn. Often others are close by.

Defying gravity, bighorns can navigate the steepest and narrowest mountainside thanks to split hooves that pinch and hold onto rocks. No nets needed for these tightrope walkers. Male bighorns, called rams, can weigh up to 250 pounds and are known for their large, curled horns, which are both a status symbol and a battle weapon. Those horns can weigh up to 30 pounds. Females, slightly smaller, are called ewes and have shorter horns. Both rams and ewes are grayish brown to dark brown in color with white patches on their rumps, muzzles and back of legs. There are five varieties of bighorn sheep in western states and Canada. Ours is called Peninsular Bighorn and is sacred to the Agua Caliente Indians. Tribe members have been proactive in working to secure their future, removing tamarisk trees, fountain grass and other invasive species that diminish the variety of vegetation.

SIGHTSEEING TIP: If you'd like a bighorn sighting guarantee, head out to The Living Desert Zoo and Gardens in Palm Desert (47900 Portola Avenue). They have a herd of them, along with 500 other wild animal species. The Living Desert is non-profit. Its 1200 acres were donated by Palm Springs pioneer Pearl McManus McCullum.

- Tahquitz Canyon -

Temple Isaiah

332 West Alejo Road, Cemetery District

Temple Isaiah opened its doors in 1956, thanks largely to Frank Sinatra. After World War II, more and more Jewish people were coming to Palm Springs, especially from Hollywood. Sinatra felt they needed a place of worship. The cost to build this temple was $4 million. Sinatra gave $2 million toward its construction; and when it was completed, he generously donated the other $2 million. Its modernist design was by E. Stewart Williams, the architect who designed Sinatra's Twin Palms house in the Movie Colony East. Sinatra was dear friends with the temple's longtime rabbi, Joseph Hurwitz. When Hurwitz died, Sinatra said, "Rabbi Joe has been an essential part of the Palm Springs community for many years, and I have grown to know this man as if he were my brother. We have been close friends for many, many years, and I love him dearly."

- Temple Isaiah -

The Block
100 West Tahquitz Canyon Way, Downtown

Tourist and inspirational author Kenny Williams is the "I" in the metal sculpture.

The Block is a small mall located at the very hub of downtown Palm Springs. Here you'll find a Starbucks, bistros, bars, upscale clothing stores, Timothy Bradley's Haus of Poke (see: Boxing Club), the Kimpton Rowan Palm Springs hotel and a dazzling view of Forever Marilyn. In the center of the plaza is "Isabelle," a gorgeous sculpture of shimmering stainless steel by quantum physicist-turned-artist Julian Voss-Andrea. "Isabelle" never looks the same from any angle, and at times appears invisible. The "PS I (Heart) You" sculpture is missing the letter "I" after PS. That's so you can be the "I" in your own photo.

Crawling atop a Kimpton Rowan balcony is one of the 10 sculptures from Czech artist David Cerney's "Babies on the Move" exhibit, which used to be across the street from the hotel on Amado Road. In 2023, after five years of being on display, "Babies on the Move" went bye-bye. This one managed to elude the moving van. On the north side of the plaza is a graffiti park. Until the 1950s, this area of town was part of Nellie Coffman's Desert Inn (See: Downtown Park). The McCallum Adobe, home to Palm Springs's first white settlers, was originally across from the Kimpton Rowan entrance at West Tahquitz Way and Belardo Road (See: McCallum Adobe). From an adobe cabin to mocha lattes, this is where it all began.

- The Block -

The Mesa Guardhouse
Palm Canyon Drive South & West El Portal

The dilapidated brick structure you see at this corner is a guardhouse, or was supposed to be. A Los Angeles developer named Edmond Fulford attempted in the 1920s to convert the then-undeveloped, mountainside The Mesa neighborhood into a gated community with only one way in and out. The only structure that was completed before the project went bust was this gatehouse. The Mesa residents love the old structure, which has historic preservation status. They even have its image on their neighborhood blade signs.

- The Mesa Guardhouse -

✳ THE MESA

The secluded Mesa neighborhood is located at the base of the San Jacinto Mountains, where it's protected from high desert winds, the late afternoon sun and tourists. Huddled together are 180 houses of all styles: Spanish, native adobe, California ranch, Art Deco, mid-century, avant-garde. Sizes vary from walled villas to cunning cottages (see: Santorini House and Ship of the Desert House).

You'll find residents of all types and styles living here, too. In the 1920s and 30s, stars like Clark Gable and Greta Garbo felt they could be alone here. In later years, Rita Hayworth lived here, as did Sony Bono and his fourth wife, Mary Whitaker. Tourist busses and vans aren't allowed into The Mesa. Even if they were, they couldn't navigate the narrow streets that dead-end at the base of the mountains. If you're lucky, you might see an endangered bighorn sheep navigating a rocky perch. Or, as I have, a bobcat walking down the middle of a street.

The main street running through The Mesa is Mesa Drive, which runs north-south. All the other streets into the neighborhood are one-ways that cross Mesa. I find it best to enter from West El Camino Way, which is where Moorten's Botanical Garden is located.

At the curvy intersection of West El Camino Way and Mesa Drive, just past Moorten's, you can see the front of the famous pink French country villa where Suzanne Somers and her husband Alan Hamel lived full-time for 44 years. To see the villa, look west to the mountainside. Best to have binoculars or be a good squinter. The compound consists of several villas connected by stone pathways. A funicular takes you from the street to the living quarters. The anti-aging celebrity said that she and Alan decided it was time to downsize, so they bought a mid-century house on Southridge near Bob Hope's house. One hopes she left her Thighmaster to the new owners, as they're going to need it. (See: Araby Cove/Palm Canyon Wash).

- The Mesa Guardhouse -

The Saguaro Palm Springs
1800 East Palm Canyon Drive, South Palm Springs

In 2012, a dowdy Holiday Inn metamorphosed into The Saguaro Palm Springs. Since we don't do dowdy in Palm Springs, it's now a dazzling panoply of pastels. You can't ignore the hotel's oversized sail shade that covers its main entrance at the corner of Sunrise Way and East Palm Canyon Drive. The sail shade is actually a "tensile shade structure," according to local **architect James Cioffi**. who designed it. "After it was put up," Cioffi told me, "a woman wrote a letter to the Desert Sun wanting it taken down, saying that it scared her."

FUN FACT

Architect James Cioffi is also responsible for the tensile shade structures at the Smoke Tree Commons on East Palm Canyon Drive (across from The Saguaro). "These were designed to look like lamps," he said, "and at night to be illuminated."

- The Saguaro Palm Springs -

✳ SPLASH LANDINGS

Just when it seems that August in the desert couldn't get any hotter, along comes Splash Palm Springs. Geared to young people, the annual event features first-rate music groups doing afternoon gigs at four hotels. Ticket holders board buses at four participating hotels (The Saguaro Palm Springs, Renaissance Hotel, Margaritaville Resort and Hyatt Palm Springs), where they are taken to the other hotels where they party, hear music, jump in the pools and drink exotic cocktails. And when the sun goes down, they get bussed to the Palm Springs Air Museum for a discotheque where they can dance under the wings of military aircraft. Pictured here are participants boarding busses at The Saguaro Palm Springs.

- The Saguaro Palm Springs -

The Willows Historic Palm Springs Inn

12 West Tahquitz Way, Historic Tennis Distric

The Willows Inn consists of two matching Italianate-style mansions, the Mead House and the Bishop house. They were designed in 1925 by Los Angeles architect William Dodd, who catered to the wealthy, in this case William Mead and Roland Bishop, who lived in Los Angeles and whose families were close. They had these Gatsby getaways built at the foot of Mount San Jacinto at the same time. The two mansions have since been combined into a boutique hotel. The Willows now owns Ojo del Desierto just up the hill.

Thomas O'Donnell Golf Club
301 North Belardo Road, Cemetery District

The 33-acre greenbelt that stretches alongside Belardo Road — from the Palm Springs Art Museum to the Wellwood Cemetery — is the members-only O'Donnell Golf Club (originally the Desert Golf Club). Of the 120-plus golf courses in the Coachella Valley, this is the very first one. Nestled against the San Jacinto Mountains, the par-35, nine-hole course opened in 1925. It's named for its founder, Thomas Arthur O'Donnell, a Texas oil magnate who began visiting Palm Springs in the 1920s for health reasons and whose house was Ojo del Desierto above the museum. O'Donnell felt the only thing missing in Palm Springs was a golf course, so, being Daddy Warbucks rich, he built himself one. The land was adjacent to Nellie Coffman's Desert Inn, where O'Donnell and his wife, Dr. Winnifred Jenny, an osteopath, would stay before building Ojo del Desierto. O'Donnell laid out the greens depending on how far he could chip and putt. Shortly before O'Donnell died in 1945, he deeded the land to the city, subject to a 99-year lease that specified the property was to be used solely as a golf course. That lease has never been broken.

- Thomas O'Donnell Golf Club -

Town & Country Center

169 North Palm Canyon Drive, Downtown

Wander down a narrow pedestrian lane between Amado Road and Tahquitz Canyon Way and you'll be stepping into the past and the future. This was the site — and will be again, thanks to preservation status — of the once glamorous Town & Country Center, which was designed in 1948 by architect Paul Revere Williams and his colleague, A. Quincy Jones. The center drew on the Spanish tradition of a narrow walkway that opens to a sunny, flower-filled courtyard. Surrounded by offices and stores, the courtyard's most dramatic feature

(still there) is a flight of floating steps that once led to a chic second-story restaurant furnished by Ray and Charles Eames. Williams, who died in 1980 at age 86, was a true pioneer: In 1923, he became the first Black architect to become a member of the American Institute of Architects. In 1957, he was inducted as the AIA's first Black fellow.

On the Indian Canyon Drive side of the Town & Country Center is a mural that the Palm Springs Police Officers Association commissioned to honor two slain officers, Jose Gilbert Vega and Lesley Zerebny, who were killed in the line of duty in 2016.

- Town & Country Center -

Triangle Inn
555 East San Lorenzo Road, Southwest Palm Springs

The Triangle Inn, originally the Impala Lodge, was built in 1958 and was post-World War II **architect Hugh Kaptur's** first project in Palm Springs. The stone and glass building immediately cemented his reputation as a mid-century desert visionary. "The Desert Modernists" book describes the Triangle Inn as "a wildly inventive building with steel beams supporting a canopy reminiscent of a lean-to." Lovingly restored, it's now a clothing-optional gay retreat. "Romantic and relaxing or fun and frisky," says the brochure. Don't assume "frisky" means pickleball.

- Triangle inn -

Truman Capote's House
853 East Paseo El Mirador, Movie Colony East

The author of "Breakfast at Tiffany's" and "In Cold Blood" owned and lived in this five-bedroom, four-bathroom mid-century house from 1968 to 1974. There's a plaque out front that says "La Cerrada," meaning the enclosure. Said his manager: "When Truman moved to Palm Springs, that was the end of him."

While in the desert, Capote had a reputation for bringing a bevy of beefcake young men to parties hosted by other celebs. According to Ebs Burnough, who directed the 2019 documentary "The Capote Tapes" (it premiered at the Palm Springs International Film

Photographer Silm Aarons photographed Truman Capote at his home in Palm Springs with his dog.

Festival) Capote had an affair here with his air-conditioning repairman that went from hot to cold. Burnough told me after the screening that Capote took the young man with him on a Mediterranean cruise aboard the Agnelli family yacht (they owned Fiat). The young man did not feel at home amongst the A-list jet setters. He especially didn't like the gourmet meals and wanted a simple baked potato. Tired of his friend's harping, Capote convinced the chef to cook him just that. But when the baked potato was served, it was a gourmet take on a baked potato. That did it. The young man demanded to be let off at the nearest port, whereupon he came directly back to Palm Springs.

UNFUN FACT

At the time of Capote's death in 1984, he had become a pitiful figure, addicted to alcohol and drugs and shunned by his society friends. When Gore Vidal heard that Truman Capote had died, he congratulated him on "a wise career move."

- Truman Capote House -

Twin Palms Estates
South Palm Springs

If I were limited to showing only one location on a tour, it would be the Twin Palms Estates neighborhood. It's where and how Palm Springs became what it is today.

The Twin Palms Estates is so called because every house has two palm trees out front. They were an eye-catching selling point when the neighborhood was developed from 1957-58. However, these 90 houses had many other more important buyer attractions.

Besides being Palm Springs's first suburb, the Twin Palms neighborhood changed the way Americans lived after World War II. When architect William Krisel and the Alexander Construction Company developed the neighborhood, they tapped into the zeitgeist of the era, that being Indoor/ outdoor living. Buyers snapped up these modernist houses within weeks after they went to market. Many bought them solely from photographs. Most were purchased as second homes. Surprisingly, they did not come with central air. They didn't need to. Unlike today, Palm Springs was a ghost town in the summer months, when temps could hit 120 degrees.

Until the arrival of modernists like Krisel, and builders like the father and son duo of George and Robert Alexander, Palm Springs was largely for the rich and famous. The modernists believed that the middle class should also be able to enjoy life here. Casual indoor-outdoor living was what young Americans were ready for, and Twin Palms delivered. The sleek, single-level houses were designed to blur the lines between indoors and outdoors: butterfly roofs,

For a 2007 remodeling job of this house, William Krisel designed a modernist front yard.

atriums, breezeways, open carports and sliding glass doors. Each house came with a pool, unheard of in a tract development. The fronts of the houses have clerestory windows, which provide privacy and light. Clerestory windows are ones placed above a roof or ceiling line.

Situated on 10,000-square foot lots, these houses originally cost between $20,000 and $30,000. To keep prices affordable to the middle class, Krisel and the Alexanders built each house post and beam. They used post-war, low-cost, standardized building materials. Krisel was determined that this suburban neighborhood was not to resemble Levittown, N.Y. He wanted each house to appear as if it had been custom built. To achieve that sleight-of-hand affect, he switched front door and footprint orientations. He varied rooflines, which included Polynesian, slanted, flat and the now iconic butterfly, which he introduced to Palm Springs — some 20 of them in Twin Palms Estates.

Choosing a floor plan wasn't difficult as each of the 1,600-square-foot houses have the same one: Living room, two bedrooms, den and two bathrooms. Kitchens were made small and open-concept because modern moms didn't need to be in front of a stove all day. And dads could be found on the patio grilling dinner.

Krisel had still another revolutionary idea for this Palm Springs neighborhood. Before, most Palm Springs houses were traditional adobe. Krisel believed color belonged in the desert. His experiment worked: Bright playful hues complemented the environment and is a signature feature of mid-century modernism.

- Twin Palms Estates -

Even though the entire Twin Palms neighborhood has Class 1 historical preservation status, only a few houses have historical plaques out front. Those that do still have their original carports. Over the years, carports were largely converted to garages.

Sci-fi author Ray Bradbury lived at 1837 South Caliente Road in Twin Palms Estates.

If the Twin Palms neighborhood as we know it hadn't been built, Palm Springs would look very different today. Because their vision proved so successful, Krisel and the Alexanders went on to build 1,240 post-and-beam houses in 12 other Palm Springs locations, doubling the city's population in the process.

The irony of Twins Palms Estates is that much of the middle-class can't afford them anymore.

FUN FACT

Architect William Krisel and builders George and Robert Alexander built 1,240 houses in Palm Springs. Besides Twin Palms Estates, other locations include Vista Las Palmas (330 houses); Ramon Rise (84 houses); Sunmor Estates (141 houses); Racquet Club Road Estates (360 houses); Steel Houses (7 houses); New Riviera Gardens (31 houses); Farrell Canyon Estates (57 houses); Golf Club Estates (52 houses); Sunrise Estates (21 houses); Green Fairway Estates (27 houses); Araby Estates (40 houses).

The Twin Palms neighborhood is located directly behind the Ocotillo Lodge on East Palm Canyon Drive. The house to the left once belonged to Debbie Reynolds and Eddie Fischer.

- Twin Palms Estates -

What to SEE in Palm Springs

Union Bank Sculpture Panels
500 South Indian Canyon Drive, Financial District

At the corner of Ramon Road and South Indian Canyon Drive is the entrance to Union Bank. More than a bank, it's the setting for two historic murals by American artist and sculptor Lawrence Tenney Stevens, a Boston-born, part-time resident of Palm Springs who died in 1972 at age 76. Stevens was a progenitor of the "Cowboy High Style" movement in art and furniture, creating large allegorical figures and stylized depictions of the American West. These terracotta bas relief sculpture panels are entitled "Palm Springs in Sculpture — Past & Future" and were dedicated in 1959 when the bank was Security First National. To our relief, they have historical protection.

- Union Bank Sculpture Panels -

Villa Paradiso
457 Villa Paradiso, Old Las Palmas

One of Las Palmas's largest, most opulent villas was constructed in 1928 by local developer Alvah Hicks for a Chicago heiress. The Moorish compound consists of four separate residences totaling 15,000 square feet of living space. Villa Paradiso's nearly four-acre property is encased by a stone wall. The walls-of-the house are 17 inches thick. Villa Paradiso's manicured park-like grounds feature abundant swimming pools and ornate fountains. A highlight of the estate is the portico between two wings of the main house, an Italian rotunda with hand-painted ceilings. There's even a classic Old Hollywood entrance: a black-and-white checkered floor that leads to a red-carpeted grand staircase — perfect for Norma Desmond to descend.

One of Villa Paradiso's guest houses was built specifically for Cary Grant by its then-owner, Charlie Rich, who also owned the Dunes Hotel in Las Vegas. Grant gave the estate its name, telling Rich that it was paradise to stay there. The guest house even has the initials A.L. on it, which stands for Archibald Leach, Grant's birth name. Other important people who dwelled here include Donald Duncan, a wealthy yo-yo manufacturer who needed a place to unwind. Ann Miller, the lacquered-haired actress and tap dancer, lived here

when she was married to Texas oilman Arthur Cameron. She told friends she was the happiest when in her Palm Springs villa. (The villa is across the street from the Dinah Shore/Leonardo DiCaprio estate and next door to Casa Adaire.)

PERSONAL NOTE: Over the course of my journalism career, I have interviewed many glamorous legends, including Ann Miller, Carol Channing, Ginger Rogers, Cher and Peggy Lee. Little did I dream that when I moved to Palm Springs, I'd be running into them again. Here I am with Ann Miller impersonator Sam Burnside, AKA Samantha Burnside.

- Villa Paradiso -

Villa Roma
Sierra Madre Drive and Avenida Granada, Indian Canyons Neighborhood

When the Villa Roma condo complex was built in 1964, Hollywood was hav-
ing a Roman love affair. Reserved seats and widescreen spectacles such as
"Cleopatra," "Ben Hur" and "Quo Vadis," were all the rage. The 1960 Rome
Summer Olympics were still on everyone's mind. While the statute in the
Louvre museum depicts the Greek goddess Aphrodite, its Roman counterpart
is Venus, so yes, that is a replica of the Venus de Milo, the Roman goddess
of love, in a rotunda outside of the complex in Canyon Corridor, across from
Canyon View Estates. Built in 1966 by James Shuler Associates, the Villa
Roma's original advertisements asserted that the design motifs included
"statuary, marble and other authentic elements brought here to blend with
supreme Romanesque architecture and landscaping." The Palm Springs City
Council granted the complex architectural preservation status in 2023, a
controversial decision because Villa Roma wasn't designed by any of our
noted mid-century architects.

Villa Serena
300 West Merito Place, Old Las Palmas

This spectacular house with the windowless, stone facade was built in 1969 for actor Laurence Harvey. He died four years later at age 45, a victim of lung cancer caused by cigarettes. The 5,500 square-foot house was last sold in 2019 for $9 million, making it the second most expensive house in Palm Springs. Bob Hope's Southridge house was the most expensive at $14 million. Villa Serena, which means serene house, was not built by our local mid-century architects. It was the vision of the Los Angeles architectural firm of Buff, Smith and Hensman. The rocky front exterior of the six-bedroom, eight-bathroom house was designed to mirror the San Jacinto Mountains. Harvey was a very private man, so the façade seems appropriate. Appropriate, too, is the ahead-of-its-time landscaping; drought-resistant desert plants growing in sand instead of grass. The one-acre lot features a pool, tennis courts and expansive gardens.

FUN FACT

Harvey is mostly remembered for playing the brainwashed Sergeant Raymond Shaw in the 1963 film, "The Manchurian Candidate." His mysterious, detached persona made him a perfect match for such early 1960s films as "Walk on the Wild Side," "Summer and Smoke" and "Room at the Top." Lawrence starred opposite Elizabeth Taylor in "Butterfield 8," for which she won her first Oscar. Lawrence and Liz remained close friends. "He was one of the people I really loved in the world," wrote Taylor after his death. "He was part of the sun for everyone who loved him and the sun is a bit dimmer."

UNFUN FACT

Unlike his estate, Harvey's life was hardly serene. He had many enemies, which he boasted about. Married three times, he was gay.

- Villa Serena -

Village Green Heritage Center
219 South Palm Canyon Drive, Downtown

Just across the street from LULU California Bistro and Las Casuelas Terraza restaurant on South Palm Canyon Drive is the Village Green Heritage Center. It consists of the McCallum Adobe, which is Palm Springs's first house for a white settler and current home to the Palm Springs Historical Society; the Cornelia White House, which is made from recycled railroad ties; and "Standing Woman," a bronze statue by Felipe Castaneda that depicts a life-size woman of American Indian heritage. The stone fountain in the center depicts traditional baskets made by the Agua Caliente women. The Village Green is dedicated to the Native Americans and pioneers who first settled the area.

✳ VILLAGEFEST

VillageFest is a nighttime market that takes place every Thursday evening along South Palm Canyon Drive, stretching a half-mile from Amado Road to Baristo Road. It's been happening since 1991, has grown to more than 200 vendors of all types, and is now held all year round. Strict standards dictate that each item sold must be at least 75% handmade. The Palm Springs Art Museum is free to the public on VillageFest nights, but online reservations are recommended.

- Village Green Heritage Center -

Walk of Stars
Downtown

There are 400-plus VIP names on the Palm Springs Walk of Stars, which was launched in 1992. More than movie stars, the names include philanthropists, politicians, pioneers and plastic surgeons. The Walk of Stars isn't confined to Palm Canyon Drive. It brooks to the Palm Springs Art Museum and onto side streets. In front of the Welwood Murray Memorial Library is a cluster of big Palm Springs legends, including Frank Sinatra and Elvis Presley. Marilyn Monroe is just across the street on South Palm Canyon Drive and Tahquitz Canyon Way. The Palm Springs Chamber of Commerce now awards stars to actors who have received awards from the Palm Springs International Film Festival. A sidewalk star costs the taxpayers nothing. The person or group doing the nominating pays about $15,000. At left, Mamie Van Doren.

FUN FACT

The first seven Walk of Stars inductees were all people who contributed to the fame of Palm Springs: Bob Hope, Ginger Rogers, Ralph Bellamy, Charles Farrell, Ruby Keeler and William Powell. The No. 1 star went to Earle Strebe, who brought movie theaters to Palm Springs. His star is directly in front of the historic Plaza Theatre.

Welwood Murray Memorial Cemetery
400-498 West Alejo Road, Cemetery District

The triangular-shaped graveyard across from Temple Isaiah's parking lot is the Welwood Murray Memorial Cemetery, named for the eponymous pioneer, horticulturalist and hotel owner. The cemetery's origins stem from 1894, after Murray's son, Erskine, died at age 27. Murray buried him here, which was on a portion of an 80-acre lot he owned at the base of Mount San Jacinto. In those days, when non-indigenous persons died, their bodies were shipped out of town by train at night to Banning. It had to be at night because the trains didn't have refrigeration. Community members began asking Murray if they could bury their dead on his property, too, and he said, yes. Before Murray's own death in 1894, he donated the lot to serve as the community's cemetery. You'll find a who's-who of Palm Springs pioneers here, including "Mother" Nellie Coffman, Ruth Hardy, Frank Bogert, Albert Frey, Cactus Slim and the White sisters. Here, too, lies Otto R. Adler, who in 1914 started Palm Springs's first newspaper. The epitaph on the grave marker of his wife, Louisa, says that she "Died of Grief Caused by a Neighbor." And this was before homeowners associations. The cemetery is full.

- Welwood Murray Memorial Cemetery -

Welwood Murray Memorial Library
100 South Palm Canyon Drive, Downtown

Architects John Porter Clark and Albert Frey designed many public buildings in Palm Springs, including this building with the green marble façade at the southeast corner of Tahquitz Canyon Way and South Palm Canyon Drive. This is the Welwood Murray Memorial Library, a historical research center. It opened in 1941 and until 1975 was Palm Springs's main public library. It is the city's oldest intact civic building. It's named for Dr. Welwood Murray, a bearded Scotsman who was many things to Palm Springs, including horticulturist and philanthropist. The one thing he wasn't was a medical doctor. The honorary title was bestowed upon him for outstanding medical service he rendered to the wounded during the Civil War.

Murray, who had settled in the desert for health reasons, purchased five acres of land in 1886 across the street from the hot springs, now the location of the Agua Caliente Cultural Plaza. At the time, there was nowhere for prospective land buyers to stay. Murray had the Indians build him a one-story rambling hotel that could accommodate 26 guests and was partly constructed of recycled railroad ties (see: Cornelia White House). He planted 22 varieties of shade and fruit trees on the land. Murray leased the hot springs from the Cahuilla and built a bathhouse there for his guests. Murray's wife, Elizabeth Erskine Murray, managed the hotel, cooked the meals and nursed the ailing who had come to Palm Springs to heal their respiratory problems.

The well-educated Murray built an adobe room at the rear of his hotel for a library where he loaned out books from his personal collection. He died in 1914 at age 81. In 1938, his son George, gave the land to Palm Springs under the condition that the city use it for a free library.

- Welwood Murray Memorial Library -

Wexler Steel Houses

East Molino Road and North Sunnyview Drive, North Palm Springs

Driving by these seven Alexander houses, you might wonder why they are a Class 1 Historic Site. They look, after all, like the other 1,237 modernist houses that the Alexander Construction Company built in Palm Springs from 1958 to 1965. Designed in 1961 by architects Donald Wexler and Richard Harrison, these three- bedroom, two-bathroom houses were experiments in stylishly affordable living, but with a twist. They're made of steel and were the first stage of a planned 38-steel-house neighborhood. Steel was to be the low-cost, durable answer to desert living. Yet only seven houses were built due to a steel strike that sent the price of the material soaring. No longer cost-effective, the experiment was halted. They were priced at $14,000. To find them, take North Indian Canyon Drive to Simms Road and turn right on Sunnyview Drive.

FUN FACT

Director Stanley Kramer, who did "It's a Mad, Mad, Mad, Mad World," owned the steel house at 3100 North Sunnyview Drive.

- Wexler Steel Houses -

✳ PRE-FABULOUS
1320 Tamarisk Road, Movie Colony East

This historic steel pre-fab house in Movie Colony East is one of
the few remaining in the United States. It was created in 1937 by
architect Howard T. Fisher, who was a pioneer in low-cost housing.
Fisher founded General Housing of Chicago to design, erect and
sell them. This one, like the others, came in eight sections and
could be assembled in two weeks. Buyers could arrange the rooms
any way they want. They cost $3,000-$4,000 each.

- Wexler Steel Houses -

William Holden Estate
1323 South Driftwood Drive, Deepwell Estates

"Solid and easy on the eyes" describes not only William Holden but his first Palm Springs residence. It's the jewel of the Deepwell neighborhood in South Palm Springs and is listed as a Class 1 Historic Site. The Oscar-winning actor lived in this five-bedroom, five-and-a-half bathroom concrete, glass and steel house from 1967 to 1977. At 4,409 square feet, it sits on an acre-plus lot. The house was built in 1955 by Palm Springs master builder Joe Pawling for George Barrett, the district attorney of Cook County, Ill., and his wife Marcia, an artist who designed the house. The Barretts wanted a place to display their collection of Far East art objects. One reason Holden bought the house is that he, too, wanted a place where he could display his collection of African and Asian objects. Neighbors say that Holden enjoyed commuting to and from Los Angeles on his black Honda motorcycle. He was known for his grapefruit margaritas, which he shared with the neighbors. Bertie, his python, liked to swim in the pool and was known to mingle with party guests. Holden's mother lived in the house next door on the north side. "The Birds" star Tippi Hedren nested in this house for a time after Holden. No python for her; she had a live-in cougar. The house was restored by owner David Jackson, a news broadcaster for KABC-TV Channel 7 in Los Angeles.

William Holden moved from here to a house at 2433 Southridge Drive, a gated community (see: Araby Cove and Palm Canyon Wash).

- William Holden Estate -

Deep Wells' bunny population increased in 1966 after Hugh Hefner bought this modernist house at 247 Manzanita Road. Playboy magazine called this Hefner's desert retreat. The 3,296-square-foot house has three bedrooms, three bathrooms, wood interiors and 11-foot ceilings. As with many modernist houses here, the front offers privacy while the back has large glass windows and doors that look onto the pool and mountains beyond. The architect was Stan Sackley, who did the stunning Jerrry Herman house in Las Palmas.

✳ DEEP WELL

The Deep Well neighborhood was an apricot ranch in the 1920s. The ranch's owner needed water to keep his investment going, and so he drilled and drilled until he found it at 630 feet below the surface, thus creating the deepest well in the Coachella Valley. In the late 1940s and early 1950s the land was converted to housing that offered spacious lots and homes of every style designed by various architects, including E. Stewart Williams, Hugh Kaptur and Donald Wexler. The neighborhood is about a square mile in circumference. Driving through its flat grid is like visiting a high-end marina where luxury yachts are moored. Deep Well is accessible via Deep Well Road, which is on the north side of South Palm Canyon East, where Elmer's restaurant is. A smorgasbord of VIPs bought here, including:

* William Wyler, 976 East San Lorenzo Road
* Jerry Lewis, 1449 Sagebrush Road
* Carmen Miranda, 1044 South Calle Rolph
* Marjorie Main, 1280 South Calle Rolphe
* Loretta Young, 1075 South Manzanita Avenue
* Jack Web, 1255 South Manzanita Avenue
* Julie London, 1297 South Manzanita Avenue
* Eva Gabor, 1509 South Manzanita Avenue

For a complete list of famous Deepwell residents see "The Best Guide Ever to Palm Springs Celebrity Homes" by Eric G. Meeks.

- William Holden Estate -

Zaddie Bunker

Welwood Murray Memorial Cemetery

400-498 West Alejo Road, Cemetery District

Zaddie Bunker in her first plane, "Zaddie's Rocking Chair". (Photograph courtesy of the Palm Springs Historical Society - All Rights Reserved)

Although there is no statue to honor Palm Springs's "flying great-grand-mother," or a star on our Walk of Fame, there was no way I was going to leave her out of this book. Zaddie Bunker is the embodiment of the pioneer spirit of the women who founded this city. She remains an inspiration for everyone today, especially as we grow older. When giving a tour, I don't have time to talk about her, but I do here. She didn't make it to the moon but came close.

A schoolteacher, Zaddie and husband Ed moved to Palm Springs from Missouri (following an unprofitable farming stint in San Jacinto) in 1913. Living in a tent and needing income, she and Ed became mechanics after taking a correspondence course. They opened Bunker's Garage in 1914, the first auto repair garage in the desert (on Main Street, now South Palm Canyon Drive, near Arenas Road, where Blaze Pizza is). There were only three cars in Palm Springs at the time. Bunker became the first woman in California to obtain a

- Zaddie Bunker -

chauffeur's license. She and Ed bought all the Palm Springs real estate they could lay their hands on, which over time made them wealthy. After their oldest of two daughters married, Ed left Zaddie for another woman. Zaddie said he traded her in for a new model. Nobody's fool, she kept the garage and all the real estate. Her house was at 494 West Hermosa Place in Old Las Palmas.

Zaddie's Rocking Chair #4 was a F-100 super saber jet.
(Photograph courtesy of the Palm Springs Historical Society - All Rights Reserved)

Bunker was always fascinated by flying but got no encouragement from Ed. With him out of her flight path, she got a pilot's license at age 60 and soloed in 1952. Her single engine, two-seater plane, "Zaddie's Rocking Chair," had its name stenciled on the fuselage. It was her first of several planes. Bunker was just revving her engines for bigger things. In 1962, at age 73, the U.S. Air Force allowed her to co-pilot an F-100 Super Sabre jet, making her one of the world's first women to break the sound barrier. On the jet's nose was stenciled "Zaddie's Rocking Chair IV." That feat earned her the nickname "Supersonic Great Grandmother," and the attention of TV's Ralph Edwards, who did a "This is Your Life" episode about her. President Nixon had her to the White House. Bunker made more news at age 74 when she competed in an air race from Arizona to California and won, beating out five male pilots.

Upon watching the 1969 Apollo 11 flight to the moon, she expressed disappointment that her application to be an astronaut aboard the ship had been denied. "I could have done it," she said. Zaddie died in 1969, a week short of her 81st birthday. She is buried in Wellwood Cemetery, which is reserved for our pioneers.

- Zaddie Bunker -

What to SEE in Palm Springs

Map of Palm Springs

- Map of Palm Springs -

Made in the USA
Las Vegas, NV
26 December 2023

83512939R00193